PASTORAL CARE
IN TIMES OF DEATH
AND DYING

PASTORAL CARE IN TIMES OF DEATH AND DYING

DANNY GODDARD

BEACON HILL PRESS
OF KANSAS CITY

Library of Congress Cataloging-in-Publication Data

Goddard, Danny, 1953-
    Pastoral care in times of death and dying / Danny Goddard.
        p. cm.
    Includes bibliographical references (p.   ).
    ISBN 978-0-8341-2436-3 (pbk.)
    1. Church work with the bereaved. I. Title.

    BV4330.G63 2009
    259'.6—dc22

                                                            2008055697

10 9 8 7 6 5 4 3 2 1

In memory of Paul and Marilyn Goddard and Tom and Juanita Waldrep, who by their examples taught me what it means to live for Jesus.

Dedicated to my beautiful wife, Sandie, and my wonderful son, Tommy. They truly have been and still are my partners in ministry to those in their times of mourning.

CONTENTS

Acknowledgments		9
Foreword		11
Preface		13
Introduction: Why Me?		15
1.	A Matter of Life and Death	19
2.	When Death Is Near	31
3.	The Phone Call	43
4.	Arrangements	55
5.	It's Personal	67
6.	The Funeral	79
7.	What Shall I Say?	91
8.	Tradition	103
9.	The Procession	115
10.	Under the Tent	127
11.	When It's Over, It's Not Over!	139
Conclusion: Ol' Buddy Boy		151
Notes		153

ACKNOWLEDGMENTS

"I thank my God through Jesus Christ for all of you"
(Rom. 1:8, NIV).

I am blessed. So many people have influenced my life, helping me to write this book. Space will not allow me to adequately thank each and every one, but I do want to mention a few people who have been extremely supportive with this endeavor.

First and foremost, I thank God who saved and sanctified me and called me into the most wonderful work in the world, pastoral ministry. Though I deserve nothing He has done for me, His grace and mercy have made it possible for me to help someone along the way.

I am so grateful for my family—my wife, son, and cousins, who have called on me to preach most of the family funerals. Each has encouraged me to put some words and thoughts to paper. My wife, Sandie, has always been my best critic and has read my manuscript and made helpful suggestions.

My sincere thanks go to Dr. Stan Toler, pastor, author, and man of God, who has believed in me from the first day we met two decades ago. I appreciate the breakfasts he bought for me at Mae's, our hangout in Yukon, Oklahoma, and the sound advice he continuously gave me throughout this project. Most of all, I value his friendship.

I must thank the funeral directors who have had enough confidence in me to recommend my ministry to those families that were without a pastor. Topping the list is Tim Adams at Mercer-Adams Funeral Service in Bethany, Oklahoma. A professional in every sense of the word and a brother in Christ, Tim has become a good friend. He has always been there for my family when we have personally needed his services, and he has been there for me, answering my questions, providing a quiet haven, and cheering me on. My appreciation also goes to the late Anton Yanda and his wife, Donna, at Yanda and Sons Funeral Home, and to Andy Shoaf and Keith Walker at Smith and Turner Mortuary, both in Yukon, Oklahoma. They continue to call me when they have families in need.

Finally, I must express my gratitude to a couple of pastors in my life. The late Dr. Bennett Dudney buried both my parents and by example taught me how to minister to a family in bereavement. He drove me 250 miles from Atlanta to Nashville, introducing me to Trevecca Nazarene College. Forever I will be indebted to him. I also want to thank my mentor, Dr. Jim Diehl, the giant in my life who showed me how to write a sermon outline, taught me how to give an altar call, and instructed me in the everyday tasks of being a pastor. Dr. Diehl became my pastor shortly after I lost my dad, and his advice and encouragement over the years have been priceless.

I humbly thank God for all of these people and the many experiences I have shared with them. Together, they have taught me how to conduct ministry in a time of need.

—Danny Goddard

FOREWORD

Danny Goddard has written a much-needed and long overdue book on pastoral care. This book is timely and will be an invaluable tool for every minister's library.

Frankly, over my forty years of pastoral ministry, I have looked for such a book and have found absolutely nothing on the subject. In retrospect, I wish this book had been written when I entered the ministry and had to conduct a funeral within two weeks of my new pastoral assignment.

The genius of this book is that it has been written by a pastor who practices what he preaches. I serve on the same district with Danny, and I have observed firsthand that his walk matches his talk. He is one of the most caring pastors that I have ever met!

As you thumb through the pages of this book, you will learn how to minister to people at the hospital, in their homes, and at the funeral service and graveside, and how to follow up after the benediction at the committal service.

Pastoral Care in Times of Death and Dying is a practical approach to meaningful ministry.

I believe it will become a signature book for the personal libraries of thousands of pastors around the world.

—Stan Toler
Pastor, Oklahoma City Trinity Church of the Nazarene

PREFACE

Author Danny Goddard refers to me as his lifelong mentor. That is joyously true, and it all started in 1976 in Atlanta and continues until this day. However, while reading the manuscript, I said out loud, "The student is now instructing his teacher!" What insights he communicates. What practical helps. What compassion. What valuable information and understanding. What appropriateness!

My father-in-law, Rev. C. E. Stanley, used to say about someone who just didn't know how to handle a sensitive or delicate situation with class, dignity, and grace, "He just doesn't know the fitness of things." We've all seen it a thousand times. There is no worst place, however, to not know the "fitness of things" than in the presence of the dying or in the services that follow. Of all people, the minister must know how to do it, say it, and communicate it correctly and with class, dignity, and grace. In *Pastoral Care in Times of Death and Dying*, Goddard covers all the bases while telling us how it should—and shouldn't—be done. I wish someone would have given me these truths forty-five years ago!

This is not a book on theory—it is a book on practical realism. Not "What I would do if I had the chance" but rather "What I've learned concerning ministry to those in death and dying across thirty years of pastoral experience." Every page reveals that Goddard has been there. And that he also "has done that." I'll listen to someone like that.

As long as there is death in our world and as long as we have services to honor and celebrate those who just died, we will need ministers of the gospel who can give guidance and speak words of comfort to scores of hurting people. How critical it is to accomplish this invaluable ministry in the right way, at the right time, and at the right place. All of us ministers need a refresher course along this line (or the original course!). Here is just such a course.

One last thing—you wouldn't think a book on the practical approach to meaningful ministry at the time of death would contain any humor. But this one does! Some of Goddard's anecdotes of true happenings will have you laughing until Kleenex is needed for the tears. But that's just like life—joy and sorrow. Birth and death. Highs and lows. Winning and losing. But through it all, Jesus is there to walk along with us. It certainly helps, however, if the pastor steps alongside to join the journey!

It's called the ministry of presence—the presence of the minister at birth, marriage, death, and a hundred events in between. Possibly the most important ministry event of all is the time of death and dying. May God help us to "be there" and to have a clear understanding of what we should or shouldn't say or do. Reading this book has caused me to want to go and become a pastor again so that "I may be there." What a ministry!

—James H. Diehl
General Superintendent, Church of the Nazarene

INTRODUCTION
WHY ME?

"'I have chosen you,' says the LORD of hosts"
(Hag. 2:23).

Everyone's an expert. Everyone has something to say. Everyone has an opinion with profound advice to offer. We all think we have the corner on various topics and that our wisdom and insight for others is invaluable. Please allow me to admit, I am no expert. After all, what gives *me* the right to attempt to guide pastors and lay ministers through such a difficult and personal thing as a person's death? Just what is it that authorizes *me* to advise people on how to minister to their loved ones throughout the intricate weeks of a terminal illness? What type of credential qualifies *me* to offer guidelines to preachers as they stand before a grieving gathering of family and friends? What makes *me* think that *I* should write a book to teach caregivers how to comfort those who are mourning their loss? My only permit is that I have been there.

I've been there as a young pastor, fresh out of college, trying to figure out this entire "ministry thing." I've been there numerous times in very sacred settings as saints of God crossed from this world to the next. I've been there, trying to answer the unanswerable questions of a young mother concerning the sudden loss of her baby during the night. My wife and I have been there to pick out a powder blue casket for a precious little boy when his young parents were just too devastated to do it themselves. I've been there to preach messages of comfort and hope to tiny groups in a funeral chapel, but also to hundreds of people in a church sanctuary. I've been there, feeling so inadequate, so insignificant, not knowing what to do or what to say. I write this book because I've been there.

Almost thirty years of pastoral ministry have passed. So many of my preacher friends seem to stay busy marrying couples, baptizing believers, and dedicating babies. Why has God entrusted to *me* the vital experience of deaths to witness, funerals to officiate, committals to perform, and folks to comfort? I often wonder if it is because I was barely out of my teen years when I lost my own parents. Those deaths, two years apart, were my first experiences of losing someone who was close. A quarter of a century has gone, yet the pictures in my mind are still extremely vivid: the chapel full of people, the long procession around the Atlanta bypass, the cold, cloudy day as we stood in a cemetery off Windy Hill Road. I can remember the things people said that brought peace and comfort. I also have never forgotten the things articulated that were totally inappropriate, even hurtful. I recall watching the attendees return to their cars, most of them I would never see again. Could it be that God wanted someone who has "been there" to try and help others who may at this time "be there"? Over these years, I have discovered that the greatest part of ministry in bereavement is one's presence.

Lazarus was such a dear friend to Jesus of Nazareth. Four days after Lazarus was dead and buried, the Lord stood outside his tomb and the Bible says, "Jesus wept" (John 11:35). Though there have been many opinions and interpretations about the theology of this short verse, I personally believe the tears of the Savior were not because of the loss of a friend but were for two hurting sisters, Mary and Martha. For a short time before raising Lazarus from the dead, Jesus was "being there" for two pitiful persons in pain.

The idea of this book has burned within my heart for most of my ministry. I love to preach the Word and invite individuals to accept Christ as their personal Savior. I get excited over seeing believers sanctified wholly and begin to live Spirit-filled lives. I thrive on encouraging local congregations toward days of great growth. But I feel that one of my stronger gifts in pastoral ministry has been to comfort both the dying and those who are left behind. Alden Sproull doesn't think this is such an easy task:

To walk with those who will soon die and be separated from us, from this life as we know it, is both demanding and draining, both awesome and painful. Such a ministry can impact the values and deepen the spirituality of the one who ministers. Through such experience the human struggle becomes more vivid. Indeed, those who minister become cosojourners in the most intimate, challenging experiences of life.[1]

A few of these chapters are clearly written to pastors and other members of the clergy as they preach and lead memorial services of all kinds. I hope, however, that most of this book will apply to anyone with the God-given opportunity to minister in a time of loss. That might be a lay minister, a caregiver, a hospice worker, or perhaps a family member or good friend. I recognize that many lay folks find themselves at times ministering to the dying and even conducting a funeral. Dr. Eugene Peterson gives us something to consider: "The Devil does some of his best work when he gets Christians to think of themselves as Christian laypersons."[2]

Ordained elder, Sunday School teacher, or timid bystander, you may be called upon to help a dying soul deal with the final days of life or you may be given the privilege of comforting grievers in their time of loss. You do not need a degree or a license but rather a heart for the hurting and a willingness to be used of God. This book is for you.

Sensing a leading of the Spirit, I pass on some of my experiences. It is my prayer that the Comforter might use these words to encourage people of all ages, of all faiths, of all places to "be there" for someone in their most difficult hour.

"Blessed be the God and Father of our Lord Jesus Christ, the Father of mercies and God of all comfort, who comforts us in all our tribulation, that we may be able to comfort those who are in any trouble, with the comfort with which we ourselves are comforted by God" (2 Cor. 1:3-4). May God bless you as you carry out your own ministry in the time of mourning.

1
A MATTER OF LIFE AND DEATH

"Whereas you do not know what will happen tomorrow.
For what is your life? It is even a vapor that appears for
a little time and then vanishes away" (James 4:14).

"Do you love Jesus today?" This was the way I greeted Bill that spring morning at Deaconess Hospital in Oklahoma City. Having complained of chest pain, he had undergone an angiogram and was now, some days later, in the pre-op area, awaiting open-heart surgery. Bill quickly answered my question with an emphatic "Yes!" He looked very healthy that day. As a matter of fact, we both laughed when he said he was feeling great and contemplating getting dressed and going home.

During the surgery, I sat with his wife, Kay, until the surgeon came out to let us know that the operation had been routine and Bill was in recovery. Once surgery is over and all is well, I usually leave the hospital. Seldom do I wait to see patients after recovery, because for the rest of the day they are usually sedated and unaware of anyone's presence. My regular habit is to visit the next afternoon when the anesthesia has worn off and all the cobwebs have cleared.

About an hour after I had left the hospital, I was having lunch at a fast-food restaurant when my cell phone rang. One of my associates was calling from the church to inform me that Kay had called and things were not going well for Bill. I threw my tacos into the trash and drove the few blocks back to the medical center, where I learned that Bill's heart had failed and the prognosis was not good. We prayed. We trusted God. We reached for faith. Ten minutes seemed like an eternity before the surgeon appeared with news neither of us wanted to hear: They had lost Bill. It was unbelievable. Only hours earlier he had looked so healthy and so full of life. Now he was gone. Life is fragile.

The apostle James compares life to a vapor, a cloud, a puff of steam (James 4:14). I once saw Dr. Jim Diehl, general superintendent in the Church of the Nazarene, demonstrate this for students in chapel at Southern Nazarene University in Bethany, Oklahoma. He explained that it's as if you and I are actors and we enter the stage from one side, go across the platform doing our act, and then depart on the other side. No one knows how long our run will take and neither does anyone know when we'll make our exit. Some stages are long and lasting, while other platforms are way too short. Life is fragile.

Since life is so delicate, I usually greet most hospital patients the same way I had addressed my friend Bill: "Do you love Jesus today?" I ask that question because I'm fishing for an answer. It is enormously important for a pastor to know where each parishioner stands with Christ. Most of the time, the response is exactly what I want to hear. There have been occasions, however, when upon realizing my sincerity a person has honestly admitted to being out-of-step with God. Such a response opens the door wide for personal counseling and prayer to help him or her get back into a proper relationship with Jesus.

Carter was a young man in his thirties who suddenly landed

in the hospital. We were not worried, though, for the problem seemed easy to correct. I visited with Carter in his hospital room a couple of times over those few days, and when all appeared that he might soon be released, I called him on the phone instead of making another personal visit. Everyone was looking forward to seeing Carter back in church. He had become such a vital part of our growing congregation. Bright and early every Sunday morning, Carter would faithfully set up chairs for children's church. I don't think anyone ever asked him to do so. It was his self-appointed job. He always came into church carrying a briefcase (we all wondered what was in that satchel!). While still in the hospital, however, something went wrong, an infection of some sort, and he was quickly moved to critical care. A day after our phone conversation, Carter was comatose and soon passed away. Our church family was devastated.

What I am trying to say is that life is extremely frail and we are never promised a single, solitary thing. Death is certainly never a part of our plans, but it is definitely a part of life, and although we do recognize that, we never seem to find a place for it. After all, there is way too much living to be done. There are people to see, places to go, things to do. It is almost as if we believe we are exempt from such a dreadful intruder, that we are, in fact, immortal. Sooner or later, however, death will find us, one and all. Emily Dickinson wrote, "Because I could not stop for Death, / He kindly stopped for me; / The carriage held but just ourselves / And immortality."[1]

One of the ugly things about death is that it is no respecter of age. As a pastor, I have personally buried two sets of infant twins, and for the same couple. I have laid to rest several other babies, as well as a six-year-old boy who drew pictures of me as I preached, artwork that is still in my files today. Such losses are so hard to accept. Children burying their parents makes better sense than vice versa, yet it happens every day.

I have also conducted funerals and memorial services for those who were in the prime of life: The head nurse of a hospital who had just recently accepted Christ, the man bitten by a mosquito that had bitten a horse that had carried eastern equine encephalitis, the auto mechanic who continually refused my offers of the gospel and died without God. Everyone who knew them agreed that each of these people was too young to die. It matters not that a family is left behind. It matters not that dreams are shattered. It matters not that the pain is at times excruciating. Death tackles us anyway and even pursues the youngest of our clans.

Not only does the loss of young people shake us, but sometimes even with adults of all ages, death comes as a shocking surprise. The sickness may not be serious. The surgery may be routine. A person may not even feel bad enough to consult a physician. And sometimes there's no illness at all—a fatal heart attack, an accident, an aneurism. Every day without warning, life for some good people who are loved and cared for by someone comes to a screeching halt and life as we know it will never be the same.

It's never just one or the other, but it's always a matter of both life *and* death. The two go hand-in-hand. It's like Laurel and Hardy. Abbott and Costello. Life and death. This revolting rendezvous with the "enemy" of our existence (1 Cor. 15:26) is a summit that's inevitable. We may be able to prolong it, but we cannot prevent it. We may choose to ignore it, but it will still come knocking on our door. Unless Jesus comes first, we will all experience some abrupt end to living. Robert Alton Harris wisely wrote, "You can be a king or a street sweeper, but everybody dances with the Grim Reaper."[2]

But please, let's not forget that prior to death there is life: days that are filled with loving, learning, and laughing; opportunities for people to receive the ministry and aid they need in their personal journey with Jesus; and chances to instill in others all we have learned along our way. Life is a precious gift from God, and we can't really talk about the dying without reference to the living.

Ministering to the Living

Although a person may be diagnosed as terminal or dying, we must remember that before death occurs, that individual is still very much alive. I think the family that is under great stress and strain sometimes gives up before the patient has officially lost the battle. Though it may be weak, his or her heart continues to beat and therefore life goes on. It is the vital task of the clergy or lay minister to help an individual along this path in a spiritual manner. My practice has been that if the person is hospitalized, either a minister from my staff or I will visit about every other day. Our calls are short, maybe ten minutes long. That's just enough time to pass pleasantries and offer a prayer for the sick.

In a hospital setting, I almost always stand, chat briefly with the patient, and then pray. Only once in over twenty-five years of pastoral ministry was my prayer refused, and that was by an elderly lady on the eve of her open-heart surgery, which, by the way, carried a poor prognosis. I am pleased to report, however, that I have found most people, regardless of their religious preference, are elated for anyone to pray with them. If the call is in a residence, I will probably sit for a very short visit, then pray.

My prayer is always positive and encouraging, thanking God for His presence, power, and ability to do the extraordinary. I mention the one who is ill by name and make the request of God's healing. Regardless of a physician's educated guess, God can and still does perform miracles. At this writing, our church is rejoicing with a young lady who has just been cleared by the surgeon who was preparing to operate in a few weeks to remove some sort of mass. The most recent tests and scans are showing that God evidently beat him to it! At the same time, we have another family that brought their dad into a city hospital from a small town three hours away. Nonresponsive, he was showing signs of a possible stroke, and doctors had all but written him off. Each in their own way prepared the family for the worst, but the church went to prayer. Within two weeks Dad was out of intensive care and in rehab. The doctors are still baffled and cannot even determine what his problem was. It is our belief that God just erased every sign of the illness with His healing touch.

James 5:15-16 says, "And the prayer of faith will save the sick, and the Lord will raise him up. . . . pray for one another, that you may be healed. The effective, fervent prayer of a righteous man avails much." The *Revised Standard Version* translates the last part of verse 16, "The prayer of a righteous man has great power in its effects," and the *New International Version* says, "The prayer of a righteous man is powerful and effective."

Christians therefore understand that God certainly has the power to miraculously heal, but sometimes, for whatever reason, divine healing is not in His will. I do believe that God intervenes on occasion, stopping that accident from happening, reversing the progression of the disease, or correcting the defect prior to birth. I also believe there are times when God chooses to allow nature to take its course, thus accepting the blame for many things for which He is not at fault. I've learned, however, that God always answers prayer. Sometimes His answer is "yes," sometimes it's "no," and many times it's "not yet." We may pray fervently for a person's healing, but instead, he or she dies. In those situations I've come to believe that death is God's way of ushering us into His presence, which is our ultimate goal. No one desires to die, yet we all want to live forever with Jesus.

Many people struggle with theodicy, the fact that bad things do happen to good people. However, God is a God who creates, not one who destroys. I will never be convinced that heartache and tragedy and painful loss are part of His perfect will. Things will happen in life that will break our hearts, and in those moments I believe the heart of God breaks right along with ours.

When praying aloud with the sick, I always request that God's personal touch be on that individual. As the sickness progresses and the signs of imminent death are more evident, my pastoral visits take place more often, eventually even every day. My daily calls will also become lengthier in the final hours. In his book *The Effective Pastor* Robert Anderson is in agreement: "When the actual deathwatch begins and it is obvious that the person will expire in a matter of hours, the pastor, a church leader, or an intimate friend of the family should be with family members at all times."[3] I'll deal more with this in the next chapter.

Ministering to the Family

Clearly, the one who is terminal is going to have the worst experience in dealing with the difficult days ahead. Sometimes there is pain and discomfort and perhaps even confusion and depression, but there is almost always the fear of the future. At the same time, as much as our attention is on the patient, we must not forget the family. There are parents and children, brothers and sisters, and other relatives to consider. They may courageously hold back emotions when around Mom or Dad, but once alone, the tears are apt to flow. It is my feeling that a minister, whether clergy or lay or even a good friend, has a tremendous responsibility to try and comfort those who can do nothing but helplessly stand by and watch. A personal call every now and then in their home would no doubt be most welcomed. Talk with them, pray with them, and send notes to them. Read God's Word to them, and encourage them. Above all, permit them to talk about their loved one, which is for them a tremendous release.

A member of our church had lost her parents many years ago. One death was sudden, while the other was lingering. This lady told my wife that when the loss is unexpected, there is a sense of shock and a terrible, painful grief. But she also said that when there is an extended, drawn-out death, the family grieves day by day and there is more of a relief than a shock at the time of passing. It's a relief in the sense that "the suffering is finally over."

As you talk with the family about their loved one, it's not a bad idea to later jot down some things that you remember them saying. Likes or dislikes. A favorite hobby or pastime. The story about the time he or she did this or that. Serious times, hilarious times. Allow them to talk, to reminisce, while you take it all in and later transfer thoughts to a notepad. File your notes away. It may be that a few weeks or months down the road you'll be asked to officiate at a funeral or memorial service. Those notes will be most helpful, not only to you, but also to others.

A Biblical Concept of Death

I think it is wise to discuss with the dying (as well as with the living) that the Bible has some things to say about death. We rightfully view death as a separation, one of body and spirit, but also a parting of loved ones. Death cowardly creeps into the homes and lives of good people and seems to rip a family member away, leaving a gaping hole and a heartache that is so heavy the bereaved are unsure whether they can survive.

Harold Ivan Smith offers a concise definition for the word "bereaved":

To be bereaved is to be *reaved*. "Reave" is a wonderful archaic English word that means to break, plunder, rob, tear apart, or deprive one of something. Thus, the griever can say, "I am reaved" and be precise because he or she has been reaved of a loved one and the tomorrows that would have been shared with that loved one.[4]

It's helpful to understand that death was never a part of God's original plan. He had created Adam and Eve to live forever in the Garden of Eden, fellowshipping with Him in the cool of the day. Could it be that the first transgression committed in that garden was not the *eating* of the forbidden fruit but the sin of just *touching* it? Though God is not quoted in scripture as saying this, Eve adds this idea in her explanation to Satan (see Gen 3:3). Temptation, lust, selfishness, sin, death—the family line was tainted. Sin was passed down through the generations. One act that took seconds resulted in the world described in Rom. 1:18-32.

This death was both physical and spiritual, a separation from the presence of the Lord. Human beings and God, who had enjoyed a personal relationship with one another, were suddenly no longer together. They had been severed from each other. Adam and Eve suddenly found themselves in a world of work and sweat, thorns and thistles, and headed for an eternal separation. Their offspring, born in the image of man, hardly reflected the image of their Creator (Gen. 5:3).

But praise God, this is not the end of the story. The amazing grace and mercy of God brought about a plan of escape so that we need not suffer forever. That plan began with the blood of animal sacrifices making atonement for the sins of the people a year at a time. The word *atonement* can be divided into syllables: *at-one-ment*. That's what these sacrifices did. It was the shedding of blood that brought human beings and God *"at-one-ment"* again. Later came Jesus, the Paschal Lamb of God, who once and for all paid the price for our sins with His very own precious blood. There are always consequences to sin, and as a result of the Fall, we still must face physical death, but thanks to the amazing, undeserved grace and mercy of God, we never need be separated from Him ever again.

Mark Twain said, "The fear of death follows from the fear of life. A man who lives fully is prepared to die at any time."[5] That may be easier said than done, but for those who are truly living the Christian life, there should be absolutely no fear of death. Imprisoned at Rome, the apostle Paul was facing possible execution, yet his attitude displayed little alarm. As a matter of fact, he was torn between living and dying. If his life was spared, Paul would continue to be helpful to others, winning lost souls to Christ Jesus, something he was definitely called to do (Acts 9:15; 13:47). On the other hand, once put to death, he would go immediately into the presence of Jesus, the eventual goal of every child of the King. The apostle believed that either way, he was unable to lose: "For to me, to live is Christ, and to die is gain" (Phil. 1:21).

Such should be the mind-set of the born again, thanks to the precious blood and resurrection of Christ. Jesus once told a sister in bereavement, "I am the resurrection and the life. He who believes in Me, though he may die, he shall live" (John 11:25). Without a doubt, this is extremely good news to proclaim to those who face their own demise, especially upon entering their final weeks of life. Read to them such scriptures as Ps. 23, John 14, and 1 Cor. 15. Show them a wonderful trilogy of Bible verses in Rom. 8:18, 28, and 38-39, and whatever you do, don't miss the descriptions of heaven in Rev. 21 and 22. We so often give more attention to a person's dying than his or her living. As an individual facing death continues to think and act and breathe, we, as ministers, friends, and family, have an awesome responsibility to help that living person to die peacefully and with dignity.

As I have been writing this chapter, Sandie, Tommy, and I have been visiting my father-in-law in a health and rehabilitation center in Oklahoma City. Last night we walked down the hallway toward Tom's room, passing a private room on the left that had attracted a small gathering. People were standing and sitting. One middle-aged lady sat in a hard wooden chair that had been pulled up next to the bed. She ever so gently patted the face of a much older woman who seemed to sink into sheets and fluffed-up pillows. She lay still. Even as we walked past the door, I could see that her face was ashen. Four or five younger people were outside the door in the hallway. It was quiet. Little was said. Lights were low. Everyone appeared to be "waiting."

Tonight after work and dinner, my wife and I made our daily trek to see her dad. We walked down that same corridor, but tonight all was different. The people of yesterday were gone. The room was tidy. The bed had been made. The patient's name was no longer on the door. I felt grateful that a little lady, whom I would later learn was ninety-one, had a great host of loved ones to not only help her die but also assist her as she lived.

Many times over the years in revival services and camp meetings I've heard Evangelist Robert Taylor exclaim, "I'm going to live until I die!" That's not a bad outlook on life. Some of us give up on life before it's ever over. Living is something we must learn how to do. Grief counseling and ministry is not just about death. It's always a matter of both life *and* death.

2
WHEN DEATH IS NEAR

"And as it is appointed for men to die once,
but after this the judgment" (Heb. 9:27).

She was elderly and only a day or so away from death. During that time, I visited that Indiana nursing home daily. On the morning of her passing, we had a good visit. Though unable to speak, she was awake and alert and she listened carefully as I read scripture and prayed. Then her eyes opened wide and she rose up in bed, looking past me and reaching, all the while with trembling lips, attempting to speak. I turned to look behind me but saw only a dingy yellowed wall. "Mrs. Garrett," I asked, "do you see something?" Continuing to reach, she stretched her arms out in excitement. I sensed this was a sacred moment. After a little while, I left. I would later learn that we lost Mrs. Garrett during the day. This preacher was convinced that a dear saint of God had seen someone from the other side on that special morning, perhaps even Jesus himself.

There was a day when these kinds of stories were not uncommon. Those who were near death would "see" and "talk" with those who had gone before. They would tell of hearing angels sing and spoke of beautiful, heavenly music. In my opinion, we seldom hear of those experiences anymore because the medical profession has learned so well how to make patients comfortable with painkilling drugs. Please understand, I am not criticizing this practice, for in most cases such medications are greatly needed and most appropriate. It is merely my observation that many of those who pass on today do so from a comatose or at least a sedated state. But every now and then, there are the Sister Garretts who seem to have a genuine encounter with the other side.

In the Final Weeks

The pastor is always needed at the time of an individual's passing. Robert C. Anderson states, "Probably there is no greater need for a pastor's ministry in a person's life than when that person experiences the death of a loved one. No other opportunity in life gives the pastor a better chance to minister to people."[1] Up to this point, I usually visit terminal patients every two to three weeks or at least send a fellow minister by. When the dying appear to be in their final weeks, I step up my calling to once or twice a week, probably alternating my visits with an associate or a lay volunteer. It is imperative that some contact be made from the church on a consistent basis.

It is understandable that friends and family members often do everything possible to refrain from reminding their loved one about his or her pending death. It's just too painful. They don't want to think about it. They don't want to talk about it. They don't want to face it. They certainly don't want their dying relative to dwell on what seems to be speeding his or her way. Their immediate desire is for their loved one to focus on life. I'll forever remember the day when my dad, who had been struggling with diabetes and kidney disease, took me into his bedroom and opened his closet door. He told me that in the event of his death, I should go to the rubber-band-bound envelopes that were on the top shelf. He said important papers were there. Not wanting to hear this kind of talk, I tried to brush him aside. After all, he was only fifty-four. A few months later, I made my own trip to his closet, alone.

Death is something from which a family wants to steer clear, but as a minister of Jesus Christ, I feel that it is my duty to do exactly the opposite. It should be the task of the clergy to intentionally bring up the subject of dying, for it is extremely imperative that a person be able to face death with a confidence that he or she is ready to meet the Savior. His or her minister or even a good friend can help with that by being brutally honest, yet with a heart of Christlike compassion.

I once flew from North Carolina to Oklahoma to visit my wife's aunt who was near death. Sandie had been there for the past few weeks. Standing in that dimly lit bedroom, I talked with Aunt Frances about the future we all knew was imminent. I shall never forget a statement she made to us that night: "I'm not scared of death—it's dying I'm afraid of." If anything has helped me in my ministry, it has been those profound words.

As Christians, we testify that we are ready for the "sweet by and by," for a "better place." We're anxious to be with loved ones who have gone before, and most of all, we are eager to look into the eyes of the One who died for us. We believe with everything in us that there is an indescribable place that has been prepared just for those who have been on a journey with Jesus. As He broke the news to His disciples that He was going away, Jesus looked into their frightened, confused eyes and spoke words that we still cherish today:

Let not your heart be troubled; you believe in God, believe also in Me. In My Father's house are many mansions; if it were not so, I would have told you. I go to prepare a place for you. And if I go and prepare a place for you, I will come again and receive you to Myself; that where I am, there you may be also.

. . . Peace I leave with you, My peace I give to you; not as the world gives do I give to you. Let not your heart be troubled, neither let it be afraid *(John 14:1-3, 27).*

Because of language like this, Christians can actually look forward to an eternity with their Lord and Savior, as well as with those they anticipate meeting again. Death is not the end, for death has been defeated (1 Cor. 15:54-57). Death is only the beginning, an unwanted, yet necessary part of life. So it isn't death that is feared by the child of God. It's this "dying" thing—that's what's scary. It's the "passing" that the dearest saints of God still seem to dread. Under great strain and stress, even Jesus wanted to bypass the dying. In Gethsemane He poured out His heart to His Heavenly Father, "If it is possible, let this cup pass from Me" (Matt. 26:39). You see, Jesus was not half God and half human. He was the God-man—a hundred percent divine and a hundred percent human. As God, He could have called for tens of thousands of angels to stop the whole thing, but as human, He suffered, bled, and died. But still, let it be said that the original desire of even Jesus was to skip the dying.

More than anything, I think the fear of dying is the fear of the unknown. What will it be like? Will I feel something? Will it hurt? Will it take long? These are the kinds of alarming questions that terrorize the minds of those who are about to cross over, the serious issues with which a dying person must grapple. A man or woman facing his or her demise may not feel comfortable discussing these concerns with those who are close, but they seem to have no qualms about opening up to their pastor or minister or even a good friend. In his great book *The Ministry of Shepherding,* Dr. Eugene L. Stowe speaks of the pastor's ministry at the time of death: "The pastor must move quickly into this time of critical need. No one else can substitute for him."[2]

I think it is healthy for the dying to state exactly how they feel, what they think, what they might expect, their personal concerns, thoughts, and fears. What a tremendous call for scripture. A minister should always have a Bible on hand when visiting the terminal. What a shame it would be to have no encouragement from the Word at such a critical moment in life. I'm well aware that many Christian workers are quite competent in quoting verses of Scripture from memory, but I believe there is something to be said for letting your friend see a passage in your Bible as you it read aloud. He or she not only can listen but also watch as you run your finger along the passage and point out the encouragement from God's Holy Word. For such purposes, I carry a New Testament that fits inside the pocket of my coat, or I may just carry it in my hand. It's never out of place, but it's rather expected of a minister.

As you sense the door beginning to open, discuss with your friend the process of dying. Let the person know that God's Word says we can actually walk *through* such a valley; that is, we can make this passage without being afraid and come out on the other side (Ps. 23:4). Praise God, we don't get stuck in the tunnel! There's a beautiful place beyond all the darkness. This is where a person's faith kicks in, so we do whatever is necessary to boost that confidence. Please understand, we must sense the prompting of the Holy Spirit before beginning such a conversation.

In the Final Days

Again, when signs are apparent that your friend is in his or her last days, the pastoral visits should be stepped up to, perhaps every other day, and then to daily. I also believe that in those last few days, as much as is possible, the call should be from the senior or lead pastor rather than a staff member. The senior pastor of a large nondenominational church was speaking along this line to a conference of Nazarene ministers in San Diego. He recalled how one of his parishioners (who was far from dying) was disgruntled because her visit during a recent hospital stay was from a staff member instead of the senior pastor. The pastor's reply was, "Oh, you don't want to be *that* sick!"

Such calls need not be lengthy. Twenty minutes or so should suffice. You are there to answer any new questions or just to be an encourager. Most of the time, a person senses a peace when the pastor is there. From personal experience, I have come to the conclusion that more often than not a person equates the presence of a minister with the presence of God. After all, He is the One we represent.

In his book *When Your People Are Grieving* Harold Ivan Smith refers to this divine-ministerial connection:

In the crises of life, many want a representative of God present. In some instances they want not just a generic representative but a particular one: you, not as a spectator, but as an active participant—one among us. In fact, often denominational affiliations, credentials, and titles mean little to the grieving. The minister is recognized as a representative of God in the "I can't believe this is happening to us" moment, in the "Let this cup pass" experience.[3]

Mrs. Gates was such a dear saint of God. We went to pastor on the coast of North Carolina and quickly became aware that Mrs. Gates was a shut-in member of the church. We also learned that she was losing her battle with cancer. Throughout that first year or so, I enjoyed some wonderful visits in her home. Time progressed, as did the disease. The final weeks turned to final days, then to final hours.

One evening the Gates family called to inform me that unconsciousness and labored breathing were leading the hospice nurse to feel that death was near. Without hesitation, I went. Walking into the house, I was immediately aware of the difficult breathing and I found my friend surrounded by her loved ones, many of whom had traveled distances to be there. I approached Mrs. Gates, called her by name, identified myself, and told her I had come to pray. My prayer was not long but adequate to acknowledge that she would be seeing her Savior very soon. I simply placed her into the hands of her loving and merciful Jesus.

After prayer, family members began to reveal that they noticed how Mrs. Gates's arduous breathing had calmed down once I began to speak. All were in awe as they realized that their loved one had ceased her struggling and that a deep peace had settled in. Again and again, they pointed out that the change had come once Mrs. Gates had heard the voice of her pastor.

Experiences like that have been repeated throughout my ministry, and each one is so humbling to me. I accept them with immense gratefulness to God. I shudder to even mention it, yet I recognize that so many times the voice of the pastor becomes the voice of God. My presence in the sickroom seems to introduce the very presence of the only One who really matters. I always feel so inadequate, yet at the same time I realize what a powerful responsibility this is. My friend Jeren Rowell explains: "Being a pastor is about *presence*. I am Christ's representative, a sign of the presence of Jesus in the lives of people I have been called to care for."[4]

In the Final Hours

In those last prolonged hours and fleeting moments, I cannot stress how extremely important it is for the pastor to be present. I cannot think of an excuse for the minister's absence, other than being out of town. Even then, once the minister who is away has been notified, he or she should make a phone call to the family. As family members are gathered in, the minister really should be a part. Our job at this point is not to be preachy or to offer advice. It is not even to quote Bible passages. We are there to wait. Though death is near, no one knows when it might in fact come. I once stood (no chairs were available) by the bedside of a saint for eight consecutive hours until she expired. Such are sacred moments. A person's never-dying soul is about to pass from one world to another. My mission is to just "be there." I seldom say a thing. I am merely a presence, one that represents God.

This is no easy task. In these last hours most of us feel that we need to say something. We sense this overwhelming urge to offer words of wisdom that will help family members deal with the moment. We think we must say something so profound that it will erase the pain and the sadness of the hour. What usually happens is that we say the wrong things. Our intentions are good, yet we open our mouths and create some awkward moments. The greatest lesson I have learned is to just be there and keep my mouth shut. Grief expert Doug Manning has said that this is the time to practice the three *h*s: hang around, hugs, and hush![5]

I did not learn in college or seminary the "magic words" that would be fitting at death. Once I sense that I am being looked upon for some kind of guidance, I usually say something such as, "There are no magic words for a time like this. There isn't anything I can say to make things better. All I know is that God hurts when we hurt, and today as our hearts break, His heart is breaking as well." Although pastors are filled with the power of God and fight devils every day, we are also human and hurt just as everyone else does.

In these times, we show compassion for a family in mourning. There are moments when the minister, without uttering a word, may even weep with those who are weeping. Jan Johnson so adequately summed it up: "I believe that we can react meaningfully to events that make our hearts ache, even when we are far away from their epicenter—by weeping with the God who weeps when humans suffer. Such weeping is also a way to 'mourn with those who mourn' (Romans 12:15)."[6]

A dying person sometimes lies in a coma, unable to communicate. Those gathered nearby may wonder about the whereabouts of their loved one. Where is that person who lives inside that motionless shell? Even then we must be extremely careful about what we say in the presence of the comatose. I heard about a woman who had been in a coma for several days. Thinking she would expire at any time, the family was present. The lady remarkably recovered and repeated to her family nearly every word they had uttered—words in argument concerning the dividing up of her belongings!

At the Time of Death

In the hospital room or nursing home unit, there is usually a nurse or a doctor who, with a stethoscope or a blood pressure cuff, will conclude that death has occurred. If in a private home without a medical person, it may be just obvious that life is no more. Once all know that their loved one has passed away, the spiritual leader may sense a proper opportunity to offer a prayer. Sometimes I ask the family members and friends to gather around the bed and to join hands. My prayer is positive, thanking God for the life that had influenced so many people and commending him or her into the hands of a just and loving God. I always pray for the family and friends and the difficult days that lie ahead. Harold Ivan Smith wrote, "The key resource in a pastor-leader's ministry with the grieving is prayer. The pastor-leader prays openly, boldly, creatively, and confidently."[7]

Once I have prayed, I back away but continue to silently "be there." There will be hugs and tears and even sobs. I offer comfort when and where I can, but for the most part, I say nothing, for I have nothing to say. When I feel the time is right, I offer information to the head of the family about what the next step might be. It has been my experience that people who do not deal with death on a regular basis have no idea about proper protocol. They usually feel overwhelmed. Sometimes I offer the information, and at other times the family member in charge will ask what needs to be done next. Although policies and procedures vary from state to state and hospital to hospital, the plan usually unfolds like this:

1. **If the deceased passed away in a hospital, sometimes there are tubes and respirators and wires that need to be removed.** Everyone may be asked to step out of the room for twenty minutes while medical paraphernalia is removed and the remains are cleaned up for the best initial viewing. The family is then invited back into the room to remain with the deceased as long as needful. I have always found hospital staff to be extremely helpful in providing privacy for this experience.

2. **Whether we are in a hospital, a rest home, or wherever, I always assure the family that there is no hurry.** They are welcome to stay together as long as they like. Many times they are awaiting a son or daughter or friend who has not yet arrived. They may still be attempting to locate someone who has not been notified. If that person is expected within an hour or two, I encourage them to linger. No one will do anything until everyone is gone.

3. **Once all are satisfied with their good-byes and are ready to leave the facility, someone from the nursing staff will call the funeral home or mortuary of choice.** The immediate family may need to discuss that decision. Perhaps they had never been faced with such a dilemma, especially if the death was sudden. Probably many families, if not most, have little familiarity with funeral homes. When I realize they are unsure about which facility to use, I usually offer such advice as, "The people at this mortuary are very kind and caring," or "I've worked with these directors many times and they have always been extremely compassionate." I try to offer just enough insight to help them in their selection.

If death has come in a private residence, once everyone is ready, someone needs to call a local funeral home. Some state laws require an ambulance to transport the body to the nearest emergency room. In the case of my dad, I was a very naive twenty-two-year-old and asked the paramedics if they were taking him to the funeral home. They explained that they had to take him to the nearest hospital first for an official pronouncement of death, and then the funeral people would be notified.

4. **As the minister speaks with the family, he or she does so in a quiet tone of voice that is suitable for the situation.** This is not the place for a loud, boisterous-voiced, Bible-thumping preacher. Respect for the family, the deceased, as well as the presence of God is the order of the moment. The tone of a person's voice can be calming and soothing or it can be harsh and hindering. This is definitely not the time or the place for the latter.

5. **I usually explain that the funeral director will probably want to meet with the family the next day.** An appointment may be scheduled by the one picking up the body, or the funeral home may phone the next of kin the following morning. I always offer to accompany families, and some have accepted, while others have kindly declined. Everyone is different. Some families welcome the aid of a minister. For others, this is an extremely private time. Either way is OK, and the minister should never be hurt or offended.

6. **Before leaving the family, I usually offer the use of the church for a funeral or memorial service and/or a dinner.** This will make things much easier for the family. Most Christians would prefer having a funeral in a church sanctuary rather than a mortuary chapel, but I have also offered our facilities to those who are without a church home.

Now this is important: *I never ever assume that I am going to preach the funeral.* The deceased may have been a faithful member of my church and I may have been their pastor for a hundred years, but the family may have a favorite preacher a thousand miles away who preached Aunt Marie's second cousin's neighbor's funeral and they want to bring him or her in for the occasion, and that's perfectly fine. Never force a family into a corner with the assumption that you'll be the one to officiate.

Now we need to understand that all the preceding is usually

the proper protocol, but sometimes this code of behavior is interrupted by special family requests. I was at Ball Memorial Hospital in Muncie, Indiana, when a dear brother in his eighties passed away. His wife, son, and daughter waited in their father's room for the undertaker to arrive. I waited with them. When the funeral director entered the room, the son announced that he wanted to help put his dad into the body bag and help take it downstairs. The rest of us followed as that young man assisted the funeral director in pushing the gurney down to the elevator that took us to the basement, then out the back door to the waiting hearse. A year or so later we relived that scene in that same hospital. This time it was Mom. The funeral director came and the young man declared, "I took Dad out of this hospital and I'm going to do the same with Mom." Away we went once again, as a hurting young man escorted the remains of his mother to the van.

Regardless of the course of action, the body eventually arrives at the mortuary. There is still much to be done before the deceased gets to a final resting place. A simple diagram of those three or four days might look something like this:

Death ❯ Arrangements ❯ Viewing ❯ Service ❯ Procession ❯ Interment ❯ Grief

Hopefully, with a pastor and funeral director working together, the next few days will be as supportive as possible for a family in grief.

3
THE PHONE CALL

"Then Jesus said to them plainly, 'Lazarus is dead'"
(John 11:14).

King David was informed of approaching visitors on foot, so he came down from his throne room and waited at the gate. David's only concern was about his son Absalom. Was he safe? Was he OK? Would he see him soon? Unfortunately, one of the runners was bearing the news that the king's son was dead. The Scripture effectively describes the regrettable scene:

Then the king was deeply moved, and went up to the chamber over the gate, and wept. And as he went, he said thus: "O my son Absalom—my son, my son Absalom—if only I had died in your place! O Absalom my son, my son!" And Joab was told, "Behold, the king is weeping and mourning for Absalom" (2 Sam. 18:33—19:1).

David had lost his son and was experiencing great grief. The reaction of the king long ago is not unlike that of people today when they receive the devastating news that a loved one is gone.

We have now progressed from "runners" to the phone call, that most unwanted interruption that comes during the day but more often than not in the middle of the night. It comes when the pastor is away at camp or on vacation. It even stops worship services.

Ministers at every level receive such calls, even denominational leaders. In an article describing "A Day in the Life of a General Superintendent," Dr. Jim Diehl tells of three messages found on his home answering machine:

> One concerned the death of a pastor in Ohio; the district wanted a letter from me to be read at his funeral the next day. I put my own phone calls on hold to write and dictate the funeral letter to the secretaries at the general superintendents' office in Kansas City. They typed and faxed it to the district superintendent's office in Ohio."[1]

It's that call no one wants. It's the one announcing that someone has died.

The first time I ever received such a call was at the age of twenty. I was leaving for work at the old Sears Catalog Distribution Center near downtown Atlanta. For me, college and a call to ministry came some six years after high school. I had spent most of those years working full time without a plan to include school. On my way out of the house that morning, I noticed my mom was lying on the couch. Since that was a rare sight, I was naturally concerned, but she assured me she was fine and insisted I go on to work.

Just after lunch that day, I was summoned to the office for an emergency phone call. The caller was my dad, who came directly to the point: "Son, your mother has died. You need to come home." At that moment my whole world caved in. I told my father that I would be there as soon as possible, and I ran through the building's second floor and into an adjoining building. Finding my supervisor, I blurted out, "My mother just died—I have to go home!" Without batting an eye, he approved my request. I ran through the packing aisles, jumping over rollers and conveyor belts. I stopped at the time clock, punched my timecard, and raced down a long flight of stairs, taking two to three steps at a time. *This can't be real,* I thought. *This has to be a dream!*

I jumped off the docks, fled across the trucking area, ran through the lighted tunnel under North Avenue, hurried up the steps into the employees' parking lot, and quickly found my car. The tears automatically came as I sped through every red light on Moreland Avenue. "She's only forty-nine," I told myself. "There must be some mistake!" I finally arrived at 462 Gift Avenue, from where a fire engine had just left. An Atlanta police car was still parked in front of our house. I rushed up the steps, through the screened-in porch, and into the living room. My grandparents, my father, my brother, and a neighbor were all standing around. A police officer was talking on our telephone. I came to the hallway and slowed down to reverently enter my mother's bedroom and a world of pain I had never known before.

I realized that there were many days when my mom did not feel well, but I was certainly unaware of her cancer. If I had known then what I know now, I would have put the disease and all those cobalt treatments together, but this cancer thing was something to which I had never been exposed. It was evidently my mother's best-kept secret, for no one in our family knew until my dad phoned her doctor that afternoon to announce her passing. Her physician even had a predicted time line of her final months noted on her chart. After spending some moments with my departed mom, the first thing I did was make that important phone call. My pastor, Rev. Bennett Dudney, and his wife, Catherine, were at the Goddard home within the hour.

What Does the Pastor Do?

When the parsonage phone rings in the wee hours of the morning, it's usually not good! Whenever I receive such a call, my practice is to stop what I am doing and go. Dr. Stan Toler describes pastoral care: "It's not just a few moments in the day, but a lifestyle. It's nurturing and committing and loving. But it is never automatic—it is always intentional."[2] It may be three o'clock in the morning, but if that's when people need you, then that's when you must get up, get dressed, and head for the hospital or nursing home or residence. My normal response is usually something such as, "I'll be there right away."

My wife will never let me forget the time when we were awakened around 2 A.M. Our telephone sits on the nightstand on my side of the bed, so I am the one who is "on duty." Fortunately, it was not a death call, but still, it was very serious. I talked with the caller for just a minute or two, hung up, and then turned over to return to my sleep. When Sandie inquired about the call, I explained, "Brother Kesterson is at the hospital in Richmond—they think he's had a heart attack." After about thirty seconds of silence, Sandie very gently probed, "Don't you think you should go?" I thought for a few seconds and finally awoke to what was going on. "Oh, yes!" I exclaimed, and jumped up to get dressed. Brother Kesterson was able to return home within several days, and we were all very grateful. There are other phone calls, however, that bring news that's much grimmer.

One of the most horrific times of my ministry was on a Sunday in Wilmington, North Carolina. I had just preached a woman's funeral on Saturday. Any kind of preaching depletes a minister of lots of energy, but a funeral seems to take a double hit. I suppose it's because of all the emotions that are involved. On leaving the cemetery that afternoon, my wife and I needed to "get away." We were spent. We drove thirty minutes down the highway to Carolina Beach, where Sandie's parents had retired and were living in a condominium across from the water. Their haven had become our hiding place, mostly on our Mondays off. On this particular day, we needed to make a rare Saturday appearance.

After a few hours of rest, we headed home to be greeted by a message on our answering machine. Church members had been looking for us, but those were the days before cell phones, so reaching us took longer. A few men from the church were overdue from a day's fishing expedition in the ocean. We rushed to the Coast Guard station to join their families in the wait. No one was at the panic stage, yet. We heard all the possible excuses, and I guess I even offered one or two myself. A few unlikely explanations made us laugh, yet inside each of us was a gnawing, growing concern. With Sunday coming, Sandie and I finally went home sometime past midnight with no word of our friends' whereabouts.

The next morning we were in Sunday School. The foursome had now been missing twenty-five hours. Sunday School ended, and we started our morning worship service. Somewhere along the way in our worship, the church telephone rang, a sound that echoed into the sanctuary. Everything stopped. A hundred and seventy people froze. It was almost as if life was in slow motion. An usher opened a side door and motioned for me. An unscheduled hymn was added, but the worshippers realized this was done to fill the time. I felt all eyes follow me as I left the platform and walked into the fellowship hall to the wall phone with the twisted cord.

The caller identified herself as a member of the local sheriff's department. She asked if I was the pastor of a certain family, the family that owned the fishing boat. I confirmed that I was, and she told me that she could not give any information except to say that "the family would need their pastor at this time." Never will I forget those words. They were so official. I asked about another young man, and she said that he had been retrieved from the ocean and was on a helicopter en route to the hospital. She was not allowed to speak of his condition.

I went back into the sanctuary and to the platform, approached the pulpit, and stood and looked at my stunned congregation. There was silence. Everyone sat on the edge of his or her pew. All were awaiting some news of their friends and fellow members. I explained that the phone call had come from the sheriff's department and that I had been called to the home of a certain family and that a member of another family was on the way to the hospital. I then asked for one of our laymen, one of our prayer warriors, to come up front and turn that service into a prayer meeting.

Though totally unrehearsed, almost exactly half the congregation followed our car to the residence and the other half went to New Hanover Memorial Hospital. My associate pastor and his wife went to the residence of a college student who was among the missing. My wife and I drove for about ten minutes, and as we arrived at the private home, a deputy sheriff's cruiser was turning into the drive from the opposite direction. I introduced myself to the deputy, and she expressed her approval of my presence. We walked in together. The fishing boat had taken on water and went down twenty-five miles out in the Atlantic. Four men were thrown into the cold waters, where they tried to stay together around a floating ice chest. About every three hours on that fateful Saturday, one of them succumbed to hypothermia except for one young man who survived a day and a night in the deep. He miraculously recovered and is now a pastor in the Church of the Nazarene.

When Is the Minister Needed, and for What?

Fortunately, "the phone call" is not always so tragic to include multiple deaths, but each call still represents the loss of life. Someone has passed away. Someone is hurting. Someone needs their pastor (or their best friend or their relative), not in the morning, not sometime next week, but right now. Even if the deceased is an individual who does not attend your church, if you are called, you go. Harold Ivan Smith writes, "Pastors can befriend grievers in their darkest despair when 'I'll never get over this!' ricochets through the canyons of their hearts."[3]

How Is the Clergy Treated?

Upon the minister's arrival, he or she is usually escorted quickly through a room full of people to the place where the body lies. That's where the immediate family waits. It has been my experience that I have almost always been welcomed with open arms. There is something comforting about the presence of a pastor. In a quiet voice, I begin to talk with the family and eventually offer to pray, going through the same progression that I mentioned in chapter 2. Still, the main thing is that I just keep quiet and "be there." As I have previously mentioned, a pastor's presence seems to be quite consoling.

A word of warning: There have been those occasions where the loss of life has left people angry and bitter, especially toward God. Such individuals feel cheated. While some react with anger, I've noticed some become quiet and withdrawn. I watched another slam his fist against a hospital door and shout words of profanity. They feel that God is the guilty party, and the recipient of their wrath is usually the minister. Personally, I have had objects thrown at me in a Fort Lauderdale, Florida, hospital room. It was in an Indiana hospital that an old saint of the church was very rude and hateful toward me. Even a best friend or the closest of kin may meet with the same reaction.

My dear friend, please understand this up front: No matter what is said or how abusive words may be, these actions must not be taken personally. These people are suffering great grief. They feel as though their very hearts have been ripped from their chests. Their entire lives have just come crashing in on top of them. We should just continue to "be there," our presence giving permission for some of their pent-up feelings to be released. I have had such people, not long after, become embarrassed for their behavior and even apologize. Their reaction is usually just that, a re-action, and is in no way indicative of how they actually feel.

What If Unavailable?

"The phone call" has come a few times when I was out of town, on vacation, away at camp, or even attending some conference or class in another state. In situations where it is just not humanly possible for me to drive to the place of death, I try to make an immediate phone call to the grieving family, expressing my condolences as well as an apology for my absence. In speaking with the family, I promise to be with them just as soon as feasible and I usually offer a prayer over the phone. There have been instances where I have called a fellow pastor in another town or state, personal friend or unknown, to go visit in my absence, something I have done as well for other ministers in the same predicament.

This might be a good place to mention that not everyone is happy with a "replacement," especially in the middle-sized church. In one of his books on church growth, Dr. Bill Sullivan points out that one of the toughest barriers for a church to break through is the 200 barrier, identifying it as one that is "stubborn."[4] People in those congregations may say they're trying to see their churches become bigger churches, yet a small-church mind-set is typically still in place. Since a senior pastor is physically unable to be everyplace at the same time, a personal visit from an associate pastor should be happily acceptable. In many circumstances, however, that is clearly not the case.

I thank God daily for my staff of ministers. They have been duly trained to handle a pastoral visit just as well as I, if not better. So many times in various places and situations I send my associates in my stead. If one of those times is a time of death, I seldom feel guilty, for I have confidence in my ministry team. I know that the grieving family will be in capable hands, and I know that I will personally make contact in other ways just as soon as possible.

Occasionally, when headed to the emergency room, I have alerted an associate pastor or two, even gone by their houses, picked them up, and taken them with me. One time when a teenager had been the late-night victim of a motorcycle accident, I brought my youth pastor along. He related so well to those teenaged sisters and friends that had gathered, so much better than I could have. To some devastated teens in a hospital corridor, Pastor Ronnie "spoke their language." Although this kind of call is not one that any minister enjoys, it is one that we all must learn to make. It's part of our ministry.

When the Minister Breaks the News

He was a grown man, married, with children. He lived in Texas; I was in Oklahoma. Most of his family members were also residents of Oklahoma, and on the weekend that he died, a family spokesperson phoned me to ask that I accompany the sisters to break the news to Mom. She lived in our town, only blocks from First Church of the Nazarene, where she had been a faithful member for many years. She was powerful in her praying and loyal in her giving but had become physically unable to attend services—she was considered one of our shut-ins.

Sandie and I met the sisters and another family member or two in front of their mother's home that Saturday morning. There in the driveway, they decided that her pastor would inform Mom of her son's passing. This dear sweet lady met us at the door, thrilled to see everyone, yet apprehensive about why we were there. We sat down in the living room, and I began to talk with her about her son, about the sudden heart attack, about the emergency room visit, then about his death. She had a little trouble processing all of this, yet finally understood that her boy was gone. She shared how proud she was of him and that she would miss him greatly, occasionally asking if the news she was hearing was correct.

These kinds of visits are never the ones in which we take pleasure, but they are clearly included in our ministerial assignment. I am always so grateful to God when I sense the presence of the Holy

Spirit and recognize that He always goes before me. He provides for me the necessary strength and guidance I need, and He always gives me the appropriate words to say. That's really all the credentials a person needs to comfort someone in his or her loss—the help and guidance of the Holy Spirit. I regularly leave these sad situations with powerful feelings of inadequacy, but at the same time, with a fulfilling sense that I have helped someone on a dark day.

Pastor or Superman?

The minister of the gospel of Jesus Christ has been entrusted with the somewhat overwhelming responsibility of caring for the dying and ministering to the mourning. In many cases, perhaps in most, the pastor's heart is broken right along with those of his or her people. It would not be a good situation, however, if everyone, including the reverend, fell apart emotionally at the loss of a life. From personal experience, I can say that there will be times when the minister will indeed weep with those who are hurting, yet he or she does not lose control. Someone must be the strong one; someone must keep some sense of order. That job usually falls to the clergy, or even to a close friend, who may still have a tear in his or her own eye. We are not expected to become Superman or Superwoman. So how does a pastor or a chaplain or a minister or a friend become a rock of support for folk that are in such need?

In Eph. 5:18 Paul's simple, but matter-of-fact, instructions to every Christian are to "be filled with the Spirit." The Greek word here for "filled" is a word with a verb tense that literally means "keep on being filled." The Bible shows us that after the initial infilling of the Spirit, such as on the Day of Pentecost (Acts 2:1-4), there are fresh infillings as needed for whatever task is at hand (4:31). There are occasions when the Spirit-filled child of the King needs a special touch of God, an exceptional boost of power or *dunamis*, the word from which we get the English "dynamite" (1:8). A preacher is never exempt. I believe such times of special infillings are definitely those days when a minister must deal with people who have experienced such loss. God so graciously empowers the family experiencing such loss, but He also does the same for the pastor or caregiver who will be ministering throughout those difficult days.

When we think of the awesome responsibility of the minister, caregiver, friend, or relative who responds to "the phone call," we realize that all of this is so much bigger than we are. These are times when we need the God who is "bigger than what's the matter," as the old timers used to say. The psalmist helps us here:

I will lift up my eyes to the hills—
From whence comes my help?
My help comes from the LORD,
Who made heaven and earth.
He will not allow your foot to be moved;
He who keeps you will not slumber.
Behold, He who keeps Israel
Shall neither slumber nor sleep.
The LORD is your keeper;
The LORD is your shade at your right hand.
The sun shall not strike you by day,
Nor the moon by night.
The LORD shall preserve you from all evil;
He shall preserve your soul.
The LORD shall preserve your going out and your coming in
From this time forth, and even forevermore *(Ps. 121:1-8)*.

Thank God for the resource of His Spirit from whom we can draw once "the phone call" has come. I am forever grateful that in those times when they call us, we can call on Him.

4
ARRANGEMENTS

"She has come beforehand to anoint My body
for burial" (Mark 14:8).

Even for the Son of God, arrangements were made beforehand for His burial. In Jesus' day, sweet-smelling fragrances were brought to the tomb of the deceased for the purpose of anointing the body (Luke 24:1). For this reason, one of the three gifts presented to the Christ child was that of myrrh, a spice used to anoint the dead (Matt. 2:11). The bearer of this gift truly was a wise man. As the royal presenters of gold and incense were proclaiming Jesus to be King and Priest, the other magus was suggesting that this Child was born to die. Some thirty years later, toward the end of Passion Week, a woman with perfume was making her own prearrangements for the death of Jesus of Nazareth (Mark 14:3-9).

When a person passes away in our day, arrangements must be made at a local funeral home or mortuary, as well as a cemetery. The process of embalming and preparing the body is included, but there is also an extensive list of other things that need to be done. Many considerate people decline to leave that chore to their family, so they visit the funeral director themselves and make their own plans in advance. It may be ten, twenty, or thirty years before they pass on, but when that time comes, the plans are made and the bill is paid. What a kind act for those left behind. There are also phenomenal financial savings when such prearrangements are made. On the other hand, there are many cases, probably most cases, where advance plans are not made and the family, in the midst of their mourning, must make the dreaded trip to the funeral parlor.

Whenever Sandie and I have moved to a new pastorate, one of the first items on my agenda has been to visit the local mortuary. I introduce myself as the new minister in town, sometimes take a tour of the facilities (if offered), and then I volunteer my services for those families without a pastor. It has always been my belief that Christian or not, anyone who has ever lived any amount of time on this earth deserves the very finest funeral. Friend or stranger, I've always considered it an honor to officiate at a person's service.

This practice did get me into an amusing situation once in Columbus, Nebraska. Having been in town about a week, I made my initial trips one afternoon to the city's two funeral homes. Although each establishment would accommodate a faith of any kind, one had the reputation of being the Protestant funeral home, while the other was considered Catholic. It was the latter that I visited first.

We happened to be in a revival campaign that same week at the Columbus Church of the Nazarene, and I guess I had "revival" on my mind. As I thanked the funeral director for his tour and shook his hand upon leaving, I said to him, "If you would ever like for me to come over and conduct a *revival*, please don't hesitate to call!" At the moment, I did not realize what I had said. I had meant "funeral," but it came out "revival." I did wonder why he had such a puzzled look on his face, but later supposed he was thinking, "If he revives 'em, I can't bury 'em!" It was about a block down the road when I realized my error, which has made my family laugh for two decades. We pastored in Columbus for five years, and though

56

I preached funerals at the other funeral home, that particular one never called me for a single funeral (not to mention any revivals)!

Making Arrangements with the Funeral Director

Shortly after an individual's passing, funeral arrangements are to be made. As I mentioned in chapter 2, an appointment is made for the family to come to the funeral facility, typically the next day after death. I usually offer to meet with them. Sometimes the minister's presence helps a family feel more comfortable as they are forced to do a business with which they are unfamiliar. The funeral director has a checklist that includes the selection of a casket from several price ranges. A vault for burial, which also comes in various styles and gauges of steel, will need to be purchased. (Interestingly, a few years ago I was admiring a beautiful teal-colored casket and mentioned to the funeral director that I had never seen one that color. He asked if I had seen the new cars in that color, and I had. That's when I learned that the colors of caskets coincided with the most popular colors of new cars for that year!)

There are limousines to rent and flowers to order. Limited finances may force a family to decide against the limos. It is perfectly acceptable for a family to prefer that pallbearers and others should drive their own cars to the final resting place. At the same time, there are those who feel that the rental cars are a wise investment, since they will eliminate the added stress of the closest relatives having to drive themselves. The immediate family typically orders the floral blanket that covers the casket. There are also optional boutonnieres for pallbearers and ministers, as well as any other flowers that may be requested. Families can do as little as possible or be as elaborate as they desire. The funeral director should be able to help the family stay within a budget.

Someone in the family should write an obituary for the newspaper, which should include the name of the deceased and the dates and places of birth and death. A paragraph about the person's occupation or at least his or her likes and interests is appropriate. The names of those who have preceded him or her in death should be listed, as well as the survivors, beginning with the next of kin. The time and place of the service should be given, unless private.

If the family chooses not to provide the deceased with a favorite suit or dress or outfit of some kind, most mortuaries have appropriate garments for sale. A certain number of death certificates will need to be secured for various reasons, and the talents of a beautician will probably be required. In many cases, a favored hairdresser is requested by the family, or the funeral home will provide the services of one they normally use. A recent photograph provided by the family will help to insure that Uncle Bob doesn't get a new hairdo after all those years of parting his hair the same old way. These and many other things are handled through the undertaker. The role of the pastor at this point is to advise his or her parishioners that their needs will be taken care of through the funeral director and that they need not stress over such concerns.

My wife and I received word that one of the children in our church had drowned while swimming in a sandpit, a popular local swimming hole. Chad's parents were ninety miles away at the time and came as soon as they were notified. We all arrived at the funeral home at the same time. The garage door of the mortuary was just going down, and the father pounded on it until it reopened. We introduced ourselves to the mortician, and he informed us that he had just returned from the hospital with the boy's body. Opening the back door to his station wagon, he allowed a young, distraught couple to identify the wet body of their six-year-old son.

A time was given for the couple to return, and they requested that we accompany them. We'll never forget that day. On the same day a baby boy had been born to another couple in the church. After crying with the young parents that had lost their son, Sandie and I left the funeral home to go to the local hospital to rejoice with the new parents and baby. For the next couple of days, we went back and forth between the happiness of a hospital room to the sadness of a funeral parlor, from the excitement of a newborn's home to the heartbreaking service of a child who was six. Sandie and I were turning our emotions on and off like flipping a light switch, an exhausting and stressful experience, to say the least.

We did meet those hurting parents in the office of the very kind and compassionate funeral director. As he began to mention the items that were needed and the kinds of decisions that were to be made, our young friends began to sob. They were just kids themselves, barely in their twenties. The young mother confessed that this was something she was absolutely unable to do and asked for Sandie and me to make all the selections. We picked out a small powder blue casket and a vault that would be adequate. A few decisions later, we consulted the couple, receiving their approval.

Mourners will want to later acknowledge the receipt of flowers and food with thank-you notes, and again, such notes are available through the funeral home. A catalog displaying samples will be shown to the family for selection and will usually include a guest registry to match. These items are often overlooked by a family during the time of bereavement. It is the job of the funeral director to take care of every detail.

Everyone knows a time of grieving is not the best time for a family to be making important decisions, especially ones that are monetary. Someone in mourning does not always think clearly. Again, my opinion is that the pastor should be present when such choices are made, since he or she can offer advice as needed. Most family members stress over these unavoidable decisions, so I usually keep interjecting such assurances as, "Your funeral director is here to take care of that. You don't have to worry about a thing."

If there is to be an interment, or burial, provision will also need to be made with a cemetery, which is usually separate from the funeral home. If a plot has not been secured in advance, a family representative will need to physically visit the grave site in order to approve the space. Even when spaces have been preselected, the family may still need to accompany the cemetery counselor to the site in order to flag the location, a chore that's inconvenient, yet crucial.

Not long ago, I had just finished a service in a cemetery mausoleum. We all stood around for a little while before I noticed some whispering going on among the funeral directors and cemetery personnel. It turned out that because of a slight difference in the spelling of last names, the wrong grave had been opened. A few members of the family standing by the opened grave had commented, "This is not where the rest of our family is buried!" Once the charts were checked and the mistake was realized, the gravediggers jumped on their backhoe and tore off down the path to another side of the cemetery. It was an awkward moment and quite an embarrassment to the cemetery officials.

Accommodations Should Accommodate

All should be done to accommodate the wishes of the family. Most people have never planned a funeral. Numerous times I have heard a griever ask, "Can we do this?" "Is it appropriate to have that?" My usual response is, "Whatever the family wants," and I have never seen a funeral director turn down a request, although I did see one fidget a bit.

We had a wonderful Samoan family in our church and their patriarch had passed away. He had always wanted to be a member of the church but had never completely made his peace with God until on his deathbed. After we had prayed for salvation, realizing he would never be in church again, I arranged for a witness and received him into membership from his hospital bed. I recall how proud he was of the membership certificate I presented to him.

A few days later, I met with his family at the funeral home. For Samoans, a funeral involves much tradition. As plans were unfolding, I remember how numerous wishes were making the funeral director a bit nervous. More pallbearers were requested than usual. The family leader wanted to do certain things that were not the ordinary. I'll never forget the look on the undertaker's face when the "parade" was mentioned. It is customary at a Samoan funeral to have a parade of ladies who come down the aisle of the sanctuary carrying flowers or fine mats. Everything is so beautiful and so meaningful, so steeped in tradition. With every request, I would say to the funeral director, "But we'll do whatever the family wants, right?" He always agreed—nervously.

Cremation or Donation

We usually talk of a funeral and interment at a cemetery, but the alternative of cremation is becoming more and more popular. It's less costly, for there might be no embalming or casket to purchase (unless a "viewing casket" is used, as I will further explain), there is no need for a cemetery plot (unless the ashes are interred), and the remains of the deceased can be moved all across the country, even around the world. I say there "might" be no embalming, that is, if it is to be a "direct cremation." My friend Tim Adams, of Mercer-Adams Funeral Services in Bethany, Oklahoma, has explained to me that if a body is embalmed for viewing prior to cremation, it is placed in a cardboard sleeve and inserted into a rental or "viewing" casket. After the service, the sleeve is removed and placed into the crematory for disposal.[1]

An urn may be purchased to house the ashes. Such receptacle can be kept at home, buried in a cemetery, or sealed in a niche in a mausoleum-type building called a columbarium. More and more mortuaries appear to be adding crematories to their places of business. Some years ago, only the big funeral home in town would have the provision to cremate. I remember once watching the undertakers of a smaller mortuary loading a van with prepared

61

bodies to take across town to the crematorium, a task they carried out every Thursday.

There are times when a family may seek the advice and perhaps even the approval of their pastor concerning cremation. I've known a few faithful Christians who were concerned about their glorified bodies on Resurrection Day. I assured them that it really makes no difference. There are good people who die every day in fires, with bodies burned beyond recognition. As Andrew Blackwood sums it up, "If a body is lost at sea or consumed in a burning building, the remains are still in the keeping of the Father God."[2] When Jesus appears in the eastern sky to rapture His Church, the bodies of saints will come from graves, from oceans, even from cremains spilled all over the globe and will instantly become glorified bodies to be reunited with their spirits that had already gone before (1 Cor. 15). I do advise people who are interested in cremation to discuss it with their family. Hopefully, everyone can reach an agreement together.

The same is true for one who has donated his or her body to science, where the body is usually taken immediately and so there may be no public viewing. At least with cremation, there can first be a viewing, then the disposal. With donation, the financial savings are possibly even greater.

Making Arrangements with the Minister

Preparations for the service need to be made with the minister. I like to set up a time to meet the family in their home or at the mortuary, and I request as many family members to be present as they would like. My purpose for this meeting is twofold: to plan the service and to hear as many stories from relatives in order to help me personalize the message. This is especially helpful when officiating at the service of a stranger. My mental checklist goes something like this:

1. **What kind of service will this be and where will it be held?** Will it be a funeral service, with the body present, or a memorial service where the body is absent? Perhaps circumstances were that the body was never found, or maybe it has been shipped out of town for another service and disposal. Will the service be held in a church or a funeral home chapel? A graveside service is also a possibility, where the entire tribute takes place under a canvas by an open grave. I have even conducted a funeral service in a hospital chapel in Muncie, Indiana. A man had lost his life in a car accident, and his spouse, who was his injured passenger, was physically unable to leave the facility. I remember how the funeral directors attempted to disguise the casket under a blanket as they brought it into the hospital corridors, a place where coffins are rarely seen.

2. **Will there be music?** Did the one being remembered have any favorite songs or hymns? Most musical selections requested are no doubt satisfactory, and sometimes they are provided on a CD or tape. Hence, I have worked many times with Elvis. I heard about one funeral where Frank Sinatra's rendition of "I Did It My Way" was played. From both a ministerial and theological standpoint, I have reservations about that one!

Did the person have a favorite soloist in the church or in the family (in case Elvis is not available)? How many songs will there be? In my opinion, one to three specials are plenty. If there are other "favorite" songs that absolutely must be part of the service, you might suggest that a couple of them be included in the musical prelude prior to the family's entrance. One song could be saved for dismissal. This way, the requested selections are being included rather than omitted.

Will there be a need for an organ or piano, or will the music be on tape? Will there be other musicians? We recently had a service where, in addition to an organ and piano, there were drums and a keyboard that fit perfectly with the worship package of blended hymns and choruses requested by the family. Often forgotten is the sound technician. Though he or she is not a singer or instrumentalist, nothing is audible without this key person. If the singers, musicians, and sound tech are to be from the church, I usually offer to contact them myself. Each of these people should be offered an honorarium of some kind.

3. **How many ministers will officiate?** It is not uncommon to have more than one minister in a funeral service. Sometimes the family likes to use the current pastor as well as the one from twenty years back, or there may be a preacher in the family. I feel as though I've been named "family minister" for our clan, since I have buried aunts, uncles, cousins, grandparents, and in-laws. If there are other ministers involved, the family's pastor has the responsibility of contacting them and agreeing with them about the task of each. When the order of service is planned, each minister's part can be separated by scripture or songs.

It may be that you were Brother McDonald's pastor sixteen years ago in another town or state and his family has asked you to come back to do the funeral. As a courtesy, you should call the present pastor of that church to let him or her know what has been requested of you. This should never be a threat to the present minister—it is merely the understanding that someone's loved one had high regards for a particular preacher.

4. **Did the deceased have a favorite scripture?** If you are conducting a service for someone who was not a religious person, chances are there are no favorite texts. It's much different, however, when the deceased was a believer. The family may recall that Grandma loved a certain scripture or that Dad liked to quote a particular passage. This may be the place to begin with finding a text for your sermon.

One of my favorite things to do is to ask to borrow the Bible of the deceased. You can learn so much about a person by looking through his or her Bible—the passages that are underlined, the notes written in the margins and flyleaves, the pages that are frequented and worn. Sometimes there are checkmarks at chapter headings to indicate the number of times that Bible was read through. Many times such a Bible is a safe keep for bookmarkers, poems, or even notes and quotes on folded envelopes or notepad pages. I will usually bring that very Bible into the pulpit, hold it up, and explain that I will be preaching that day from Sister Simmons's very own Bible. This has always proven to bring comfort to the family.

5. **Will there be anything else in the service?** So many other things can be incorporated into a funeral service, everything from poems and personal eulogies to video or slide presentations. It is best that the minister be told of all such plans in this family meeting in order to strategically place each part in the service. I know from personal experience that when the family stays up the previous night past midnight reminiscing of days gone by, someone will think of a particular story or something that would certainly fit into the service. So I am never surprised when, just moments before the service is to begin, word comes that a close relative will have some things to say. Of course, our answer is always, "Whatever the family would like."

6. **Will there be viewing before or after the service, or at both times?** This is good to know up front so that you can anticipate what will take place at the close of the service. Since the family generally gathers in a side room to await an escort into the service, the minister and family of the deceased are not usually nearby for a preservice viewing. However, the family may want to request this for those coming in a bit early, something that I will cover in a later chapter. It's not a bad idea for the minister to make a personal visit into the sanctuary once funeral personnel have arrived. Amid all the breathtaking floral displays, room must be left for the minister

to ascend and descend the steps of the platform, as well as a place for him or her to stand after the service has concluded. I've learned from experience that a preacher can be unintentionally left in the bushes, so I like to personally check this prior to anyone's arrival.

7. **What will follow the service?** Again, the one officiating will need a plan in mind once the service is over. Arrangements with the funeral director should help relieve a family of needless worry. In short, professionals are being paid to carry out every detail. The minister-family meeting is to help the preacher arrange the service in a simple but meaningful fashion. It is now time for the pastor to write his or her sermon, and unlike preaching from Sunday to Sunday, this time he or she only has a day or so to get to the finished product.

5
IT'S PERSONAL

"Precious in the sight of the LORD is the death
of His saints" (Ps. 116:15).

The psalmist made it quite clear that death is an extremely personal thing—at least it is to God. The God who knows the number of hairs on our heads is also interested in and aware of a person's death. The God who knows when every sparrow falls to the earth also knows when one of His own children has died. After all, He is the One who created us and He is the One who knows how, when, and from where each of us will leave this earth.

Through the prophet Jeremiah, God promised, "'For I know the plans I have for you,' declares the LORD, 'plans to prosper you and not to harm you, plans to give you hope and a future'" (Jer. 29:11, NIV). Regardless of who we are or how we were raised or where we might live, God has a redemptive plan that includes each of us. Unfortunately, not everyone seeks that plan. Some have absolutely no interest in God's direction for their lives. They have their own agendas with specific destinations already in mind.

Whether or not we are interested in the spiritual, God is still tugging on our hearts and continually trying to persuade us to go

His way. Too many times we choose to go our own route and dare to ask God to bless it. Jesus told Andrew and Philip, "If anyone serves Me, let him follow Me; and where I am, there My servant will be also" (John 12:26). Our Lord doesn't follow us, we follow Him. He promises to bless us, but in the place where He is, not the spot where we want to be.

Since life and death are both so incredibly personal, a person's funeral should be no different. Quite some time ago, I decided that I had attended too many impersonal funeral services—tributes where the deceased was hardly mentioned. I have listened to preachers exhort on the twenty-third Psalm or explain in great speculative detail why "Jesus wept" (John 11:35). I've heard ministers present tremendous treatises on how everyone is born to die. I have observed how some messages were nothing more than verses of Scripture linked together like hot dogs in a butcher's shop. A. Wolfelt called such services "generic funerals" or "cookie cutter ceremonies that leave you feeling like you may as well have been at a stranger's funeral."[1] O. Duane Weeks goes farther:

> When funeral services have no personal significance to the survivors, they are of little benefit and may, in fact, be harmful. A clergyman once boasted to a funeral service class that he had conducted more than a thousand funerals, using an identical service for each except for changing the name of the deceased and the dates of birth and death.
>
> This is, of course, an extreme example of laziness and mediocrity, but caregivers are too often inclined to plan death rituals that are familiar or helpful to them, rather than to the survivors."[2]

But what about Brother Scarpa or Cousin Nita or Uncle Ansley? What about the guest of honor, the person who has brought the crowd together? Why is nothing said about the one who lived so few or so many years and so powerfully influenced the life of someone? I vowed and declared early in my ministry that in every funeral service I would preach the gospel, but I would also have something uplifting and encouraging to say about the one who has departed. Let us never forget that he or she is the reason everyone is there.

So how does a preacher "personalize" a funeral sermon, especially those messages for the ones you didn't even know? Here are a few thoughts that have been helpful to me in sermon preparation for a funeral or memorial service:

1. **Do research on the deceased.** As previously mentioned, when you meet with the family, you should be prepared to take notes. Begin by asking pertinent questions to open up a time of reminiscing. You'll most likely find that people will weep one minute, then laugh the next. This session usually turns out to be a very heartwarming and therapeutic experience that leaves everyone feeling just a little bit better. As the anecdotes and remembrances begin to pour, the minister just listens and jots down words, phrases, and quotes that he or she can later use to make that person "live" again. And please, Reverend, focus only on the positive.

A North Carolina funeral director called me to officiate at a service for a pastorless person with whom I was not acquainted. All I was told was that he had been a very wealthy man, the owner of a small oil company. The mortician gave me two phone numbers, one for an aunt, and I believe the other was for a cousin. I phoned the first, introducing myself and offering my personal condolences. I asked if she would mind telling me anything about her nephew that might help me to know him. She responded, "Yeah, I'll tell you about him—he was a miser, he was a crook, he took advantage of everyone," and on and on she ranted. I finally thanked her for her trouble and hung up. I called the next number, that of the cousin, and was promptly told, "We're all better off without him!" I didn't stay on the phone very long with him, either. Since the departed didn't have much of a fan club, I decided to go ahead without any help from his "friends." I just preached the gospel and tried to continuously point out how much God had loved this man and how much God loves us! We must always find the positive side, even if it is a stretch to do so.

2. **Pray for God's direction.** In every situation, the first thing the preacher should do is pray. Pray for God's comfort for the family and friends but also pray for God's help for you. As Harold Ivan Smith has said, "The historic advice 'Take it to the Lord in prayer' is wise for grievers and pastors alike. From the first moments of notification, the pastor-leader is praying, *Lord, guide me.*"[3] If you're the preacher, you have the awesome responsibility of putting together words from God's Word that are meant to comfort and provide peace and closure. If divine guidance is ever needed by you in this whole funeral process, it is during this preparation of the sermon.

As mentioned in chapter 4, a good place to begin is with the personal Bible of the deceased. If the departed was a Christian, ask the immediate family if you might borrow his or her Bible. Assure them that it will be returned as soon as the service is over. Once alone, sit down with that book and leaf through it, looking for verses that may be underlined or marked in such a way as to suggest that they may be favorite texts. If a Bible is not available, especially as is the case of those who were without Christ, begin to seek God for a text, incessantly keeping the deceased in mind.

I once preached the funeral of a retired baker named Jerry. Everyone in town remembered him as the one who used to make the doughnuts at the little shop on Main Street. With that in mind, I used the text "The kingdom of heaven is like leaven, which a woman took and hid in three measures of meal till it was all leavened" (Matt. 13:33). I called that message "Jerry's Leaven." Another funeral was for a man who had spent his life as a merchant marine on the sea. My text was "Those who go down to the sea in ships, who do business on great waters, they see the works of the LORD, and His wonders in the deep" (Ps. 107:23-24).

More recently, I officiated at a memorial service for a man whose body was cremated. He and his ex-wife had been divorced for thirty-seven years, yet throughout the years they had remained close friends. She told me of his love for reading mystery novels. Did you know the word "mystery" appears twenty-one times in the NKJV? As a tiny gathering of people stared at a brass urn on a wooden pedestal, I preached about the mystery of life and someday discovering the ultimate mystery, that of eternal life with Jesus. Try your best to match verses of Scripture with the individual being remembered. It will be most meaningful to everyone in attendance.

Such personal messages are only birthed under the inspiration of Almighty God. You'll always need the mind of Christ, the thoughts of the Father, the aid of the Spirit. You must know that when you write those creative words and phrases, you are being used and motivated by Him. This is a task the preacher will never want to begin alone. It absolutely must be a God-thing.

3. Find some privacy. My usual pattern is to find a quiet place where I can be alone, and it's there that I begin putting notes on a legal pad. I don't usually go to my study at the church for this first stage of sermon preparation. There are just too many phone calls and voices in the hallway and people stopping by. Often I will stay up late at our dining-room table after everyone else has gone to bed. I might go to a restaurant during the day and hide in a corner booth with a tall Diet Dr Pepper. It is imperative that you find a silent, secluded place to collect your thoughts. When a preacher is working on a funeral, all else comes to a stop. The funeral always takes top priority.

I was preaching a revival at the other end of the state when "the phone call" came concerning my 84-year-old father-in-law, Tom Waldrep. I quickly checked out of the hotel and hit the interstate for a two-hour drive. As I continued toward Oklahoma City, the thoughts kept flooding my mind. While alone on the highway, I put much of the sermon together in my head.

A day or so of funeral arrangements later, I needed a quiet place for putting some thoughts on paper. Just about every Monday for eleven weeks, I had sat by my father-in-law's hospital bed with a book or a laptop or a legal pad. I was able to get so much accomplished, including sermons written, on my day off, just sitting with Tom. On this particular day, I decided to go to the funeral home and into Tom's state room. For over three hours, with a background of beautiful, peaceful music and the sound of the babbling fountain from around the corner in the foyer, I sat by his casket and filled up almost two legal pages of notes for my message.

Once I have a text from God and some notes for personalization, I usually go to my study at the church and close the door. This may be the day before or the morning of the service. If it is the same day of the funeral, I usually arrive at the church very early. Trying to keep interruptions to a minimum, I ask my secretary to hold all phone calls unless they are from the funeral home, my own family, or that of the deceased. With the clock ticking away, I must be focused on the task at hand and be able to think clearly from start to finish. I never emerge from my office until the sermon is written, the outline typed and printed, and even preached at least once in the privacy of my study.

4. Keep it simple. It is a rare thing for funeral attendees to have Bibles with them. Since they will only have some worn-out tissues, don't expect them to follow along in the scripture. The text should never be a long passage; it should be short, perhaps one to two verses long. I like to find at least three points that I can lift from the text and apply to the deceased—three things that can be easily recalled. I'll announce the first truth of the scripture, point number one, and I'll read the first part of the text. A minute or two will be spent expounding that part of the verse, putting it into its proper context. Then I will bring the one who has died into the picture, applying that part of the verse to him or her. This will be done with each and every point. The Bible is being preached while the one who is gone is continually kept in front of the congregation. This three-point style probably won't fit with those who are strictly narrative preachers, but this is what I normally do.

A funeral sermon is not the place for great theological instruction. People are not in the mood to have their brains stretched or to learn some tremendous truth from the Word of God. They don't want to think. Many of them are in a fog, a daze. They may still be in denial and feel as though they are in a bad dream. What they need is comfort and peace and closure, all of which can be accomplished with plain but powerful truths presented from God's Word in a very simplified way.

5. Preach reverently. When I preach in my church on Sunday, I am quite animated, seldom staying behind the pulpit, moving around on the platform. My voice is louder. My entire body goes into the presentation. I'm not a teacher or a lecturer. I am a preacher. It is my God-called task to make the scripture come alive. I love the verse that says Jesus "preached the word to them" (Mark 2:2). I'm so weary of ministers "sharing"—I want to hear someone "preach" the Word of God! Before I enter the pulpit, I always pray that God will help me to preach with fervency and fire! Though that is my usual preaching style, I feel that a funeral or memorial sermon should be presented without quite the same level of energy.

A funeral is no forum for a preacher to yell and scream, rant and rave, fling arms wildly, jump pews or swing from chandeliers! It is a time, rather, for comfort and peace to be gently and purposefully extended to a gathering of hurting people. We should feel exactly the same way Christ did when He saw His people hurting and helpless. "But when He saw the multitudes, He was moved with compassion for them, because they were weary and scattered, like sheep having no shepherd" (Matt. 9:36). For this reason, while preaching a funeral or memorial service message, I plant myself firmly behind the pulpit. Though I try to use inflection in my voice, I don't preach with the same loudness that I might on Sunday morning. I try to keep smiling, and I preach with a comforting, yet convincing tone of voice.

6. **Don't be afraid to use humor.** Some people have the idea that we cannot laugh at a memorial service. I suppose they feel it is disrespectful. I strongly disagree. As a matter of fact, I purposely look and listen for humorous stories, especially those about the deceased. Such stories seem to relax everyone and help them to remember the good times and "see" that person "alive" once again. Dr. Les Parrott III says that humor helps a person deal with suffering and loss: "Humor helps us cope—not just with the trivial events but even with the tragic."[4] In an article he wrote for *Holiness Today*, Parrott mentions Charlie Chaplin, his childhood in the poorest section of London, his mother's serious mental illness, and his father's death from alcoholism when Charlie was only five. "Laughter was Chaplin's tool to cope with life's losses," reports Parrott. "When he eats a boiled leather shoe for dinner in his classic film, *Gold Rush*, it's more than a humorous scene. It is an act of human triumph, a monument to the coping power of humor."[5]

So use the comical stories that members of the family tell you. Relate your own personal experiences with the one being honored, especially if you are the brunt of the joke. And whatever you do, be sure to use humor in a tasteful way. Pick and choose only those amusing anecdotes that present the deceased in a pleasing light.

Robert Anderson agrees: "Though a funeral ought not to consist of a series of jokes, it is not at all out of line at a funeral to share bits of humor that are representative of a person's life and that may help the bereaved to remember him as he actually was. Such humor, shared in taste, may provide a heartwarming experience for those who are mourning."[6]

7. **Remember, the funeral is not for the dead.** A young woman in one of my pastorates was dreadfully afraid of funerals, mortuaries, anything to do with death. She would bring food to the church and be helpful, but she refused to attend a funeral. One day we were discussing this and she told me that whenever she dies, she does not want a funeral. Without hesitation, I exclaimed, "That's the most selfish thing I've ever heard!" I could see she was taken aback by my comment, but it opened the door for me to explain something to her. I told her that though it would be her funeral, it would not really be for her but for everyone else—her family, her friends, all those who would suffer her loss. A funeral or memorial service is closure for those left behind. It's a way of working through the pain and the grief. It's a service that allows the Holy Spirit, the Comforter, to bring tranquillity in the midst of mourning, and it allows people to say their good-byes.

There have been ministers who have refused the opportunity to officiate at a funeral because they thought the deceased was an unbeliever. I'll grant you, preaching a service for a Christian is much easier than for a nonbeliever, but even if the spiritual question is uncertain, the preacher must keep in mind that he or she is preaching to a congregation, not to a dead body. It's too late for the deceased. There is nothing we can say that will change his or her eternity, but what a chance to proclaim the message of the gospel to an assembly of friends and family, some of whom may be without the Lord.

8. **Make your message tastefully evangelistic.** A funeral service is not the time to preach a hellfire and brimstone message to force everyone in attendance to choose an eternal home. A minister should never be guilty of playing with people's emotions. The

general superintendent who ordained me, Dr. Eugene Stowe, says, "The one inviolable rule is that the message must not be a hard-sell evangelistic appeal! This is neither the time nor the place to exploit the already overwrought emotions of the bereaved."[7] At the same time, a funeral is often the only thing that will bring some people to church. My plan has always been to include in my message a taste, a hint of evangelism.

Throughout the message, the gospel can be presented in a non-threatening way—short statements here and there, reminders of how the Christian deceased believed or acted. Most of my funeral sermons end with a statement or two like this: "The spotlight is not on Brother Harold today, but rather it's on us. We have the assurance that he has reached his goal. He has made it to the other side. Now you and I must live our lives in such a way that will guarantee our being together again someday." Put this way, those without Christ are not coerced into making a decision on impulse, yet they are left with something to seriously consider.

I like Dr. Anderson's thoughts on this:

It is not only proper but desirable that the funeral sermon always contain the gospel message in clear terms. The message should be presented in a polite, nonthreatening manner. It is not right to harangue the bereaved or attempt scare tactics to propel them into the kingdom of God. A simple explanation of the gospel message, including the necessity for a person to commit his life personally to Jesus Christ as Lord and Savior, and a simple step-by-step description of how a person may do that will suffice.[8]

Personally, I would have to be certain that God was leading me to give an invitation. I cannot recall ever doing that, but I seldom miss the opportunity to leave something for contemplation.

My dear minister friend, I close this chapter with one urgent request: Do away with any generic funeral sermon you might have in a dusty file drawer and write a fresh message each time. As Duane Weeks puts it, "To be helpful, a death ritual must have some value to the survivors. To have value, the ritual must also have meaning. And to have meaning, the ritual must be personal."[9] Make your message about the person being remembered. Please don't exhort on and on about how worms are going to destroy that body, as I was shocked to hear one pastor do. Believe me, that is the last thing the family wants to hear. Make it personal. Keep it simple. Allow the deceased to "live again," at least for twenty minutes on a difficult day. Allow God to speak through you to touch some aching hearts. Though their loved one is gone, those dear people should go from that service with him or her "alive" in their hearts. You and I under the anointing of the Spirit are the ones who make that possible.

Not long ago, I received "the phone call" concerning the passing of a professional wrestler of the fifties and sixties who worked under the ring name Sputnik Monroe. We had been personal friends for over forty years. As a thirteen-year-old, I made three road trips to wrestling matches in Florida with him and a few other wrestlers. I am so glad that my family had paid him a visit at his home in Houston two years before his death, allowing my son the opportunity to meet him. As a matter of fact, Monroe, who was then seventy-five years old, demonstrated wrestling holds on Tommy during our short visit. Even at that time, his health had been in decline, and as we were preparing to leave, he asked me to pray for him. I stood, put my hand on the shoulder of one of the meanest wrestlers in the business, one who had been my childhood hero, and I prayed for God to make a difference.

My friend passed away of natural causes at the age of seventy-seven. His body was cremated in Florida, and the cremains were delivered to Louisiana for burial. I was honored when asked by his family to conduct his graveside service at a national cemetery. Having learned that he had made his peace with God through a priest only two weeks prior to his passing, I used Heb. 12:1-2 as a text: "Therefore we also, since we are surrounded by so great a cloud of witnesses, let us lay aside every weight, and the sin which so easily ensnares us, and let us run with endurance the race that is set before us, looking unto Jesus . . . " I mentioned how at some point in our lives, most of the sixty people in attendance had sat in the bleachers at a wrestling arena, cheering for Sputnik Monroe. But then I explained that because of his decision two weeks earlier, the wrestler himself was now in the stands cheering for us. It all seemed to fit, and kind comments were made afterward. As I sat on a small jet to Houston later that evening, I was content knowing that the Spirit had used me once again to help some people in pain. My preacher friend, please get rid of the canned sermons and personalize your memorial messages. It will make a huge difference to someone.

6
THE FUNERAL

"Jesus arrived at the rabbi's home and saw the noisy
crowds and heard the funeral music" (Matt. 9:23, TLB).

Pastor Joshua took the teens outside on a Wednesday evening in
May to attend the "funeral" of the old Dodge Dart. The youth of our
church had purchased the rusty green 1974 automobile for a song,
intending to use it for promotions at high school football games, local parades, and other such events that would attract young people.
The group's leadership even took the time (but not the expense)
of painting the vehicle an ugly green on a warm Oklahoma night.
They performed this task under a street lamp, with a paintbrush,
while mosquitoes and gnats were attracted to the light, some of
them taking up permanent residence on the wet paint. They hoped
that the old heap would become a symbol, an icon, one that high
schoolers would identify with the student ministries of Yukon First
Church of the Nazarene.

I think the old car did make an appearance or two and even
found its way into a few youth-produced videos, but its road life
was just too far gone. The engine coughed and choked for the last
time. One of the tires was flat. The old Dodge Dart had seen its
best days.

The newly revised plan was to beat the car beyond recognition with a sledgehammer at a dollar-a-lick teen fund-raiser. We were now within days of the old Dart's final ride to a place in Oklahoma City where it would be lifted by a huge magnet, dropped into a giant shredder, and turned into tin foil. But the kids were attached to it. The old car had found a parking place in their hearts. We knew we couldn't just discard it and move forward as if nothing had happened. So on a Wednesday night Student Ministries Pastor Joshua Lindley set up steel folding chairs encircling the old Dodge just outside the west end of the church building. He provided a funeral folder complete with an obituary, listing the year of the vehicle's assembly and the year of its demise. He then gave the teens a chance to publicly share their personal, fond memories of the Dart.

One by one, the teens eulogized that old beat-up Dodge. Pastor Joshua explained that the worn-out vehicle would be turned into scrap metal that could be used for something new. He then shifted gears, using the occasion to speak to his hearers about the death and resurrection of Jesus and how we can enjoy new life in Christ. When I heard what was going on, I thought to myself, *That youth minister definitely has the right idea about conducting a funeral!*

A few days later I was busy at my desk in my study when I heard the rumbling sound of a rather loud tow truck in the parking lot. Though the temptation was great, I refrained from peeking through the blinds, for I assumed the sight would be too hard to behold. I knew the wrecker had come to take the old green Dart to its final resting place.

According to Brother Webster, a funeral is "a ceremony at which a dead person is buried or cremated."[1] Such a service is a significant event to remember the departed, reflect on good times, and challenge the living. Though the attention is usually on the deceased, the service is never for him or her but rather for those who are left behind, to help heartsick mourners come to a closure and cope with their grief.

Of what should a funeral or memorial service consist? Theologian Thomas Oden believes a well-rounded funeral should include thanksgiving, intercession, recollection, witness, and committal, to which I certainly agree.[2] It is a service where we should always express gratitude to God for the one who is gone and for all the lives he or she had touched. We should pray, invoking God's presence and asking for strength for those in sorrow during the difficult hour. Hopefully, the recollection of stories and anecdotes of days gone by will help every attendee remember their friend or loved one. A funeral is the perfect occasion to interject a taste of evangelism and witness about what our Savior has in store for anyone who believes. And finally, it is the official setting to commit the soul of the departed to his or her Creator.

Recently surfing the Web for information on funerals, I came across a handbook of policies concerning a particular church that will remain nameless. It was all most interesting, yet somewhat so official, so impersonal, so bland and boring. For instance, there was the rule that allowed a funeral to be scheduled in that church only after verification that the deceased had been baptized. The book goes on to say that there may only be three musical selections in a funeral service and that all three should unquestionably be from the hymnal. Permission may be granted for friends to offer eulogies, but only after the pastor has been notified. Six pallbearers must be named and will sit together on a designated pew. On and on it goes, until the policy booklet boldly concludes with the solicitation of a donation. It was one of the coldest and most insensitive documents I have ever read. Regardless of the faith of the deceased, let's provide for them the most meaningful funeral possible. It's the last official tribute for a fellow human being.

We've discussed the funeral sermon and we've looked at ways to make the message more personal. Now let's turn our attention to the funeral service itself. In an effort to cover every angle, we will examine it through the five Ws of journalism—Who? What? When? Where? and Why?

1. Who? There are a couple of "whos" to address, with the first and most important being the guest of honor—the deceased. It cannot be stated enough that both the funeral service and the funeral message should be as personal as possible. Please don't ignore the deceased and don't pretend that nothing has happened, the criticism leveled at many a memorial. When Dr. Dan Boone was called upon to officiate at the funeral of a bright and promising young mother who was also his children's pastor, he addressed the mourners with the most honest and appropriate words he could muster: "This stinks!"[3] There is no need to tiptoe around the reason you're gathered together. Why should you? Why would you? It is no secret that someone has died, so address it up front: "We're here this afternoon to remember Granvil and to celebrate his life, but this was definitely not the plan of a loving God!"

The other "who" consists of the hearers—the audience, the congregation, the mourners. This group is made up of family, friends, and even mere acquaintances. Sometimes there are those who had never met the deceased, yet for some reason felt drawn to attend his or her service. Hopefully, you won't have vagrants in attendance. While I was serving in one town, the local pastors had to address a growing concern at the monthly meeting of our ministerial alliance. A particular man had been spotted attending all the funeral dinners in town over a period of several weeks. The large church pastor would conduct funerals once or twice a week and had noticed this one individual at most of the feasts. The man evidently had been checking out the obituary section of the local newspaper and tracking down a free lunch. As I recall, I think we arranged for him to be fed elsewhere, offering ministry to him but also preserving respect for the deceased.

So then, just what is our responsibility to the grievers at a funeral? A veteran pastor once said to me just before he and I went out of my study to officiate at a funeral, "I never have figured out what we're supposed to do at these things!" I think he was expressing to me the feeling of inadequacy that most pastors feel before any kind of service, but especially one of this type. The day a minister feels overly confident in himself is the day to begin selling tacos down the street or doing something else. We must always humbly rely upon the Holy Spirit to anoint, help, and guide us.

Clearly, a funeral is not a good thing. I have on occasion even begun a service with words such as, "This is the last place we want to be today." Though we do our very best to make it a meaningful experience, a memorial service is a sad occasion. It hurts. It rips at the heart. It clobbers us right between the eyes with the painful feeling of finality. Yet we ministers and other encouragers have the enormous responsibility of attempting to help people feel better and find some peace in the midst of all the chaos. They will no doubt still leave the service with a heavy, breaking heart, but hopefully, they will go away with a sense of having been part of a tremendous tribute to a man or woman, boy or girl, who had made a difference in the life of someone.

2. What? What kind of service will this be? Will it be a funeral, a memorial service, or a graveside gathering? A *funeral service* usually means the body is present. It may be a closed- or open-casket service, or there may be ashes in an urn, but nevertheless, the remains are there. Typically, a *memorial service* is a service for someone whose remains are not available, yet that person is being openly remembered. Aside from many individual funerals, the public services for the victims of the Oklahoma City bombing or for those of 9/11 were memorial services, prepared experiences to

help our nation remember. A *graveside service* is simply a funeral at an open grave or in the mausoleum of a cemetery and is normally a shorter service.

When officiating in a church or chapel, I usually meet with the family about five minutes prior to the service. I briefly explain that the funeral director will be lining them up momentarily to lead them into the sanctuary, chapel, or family viewing room. After reminding them that our purpose is to celebrate Mom's life, I pray for them, asking God's Holy Spirit to especially help them over the next few hours. I depart, leaving them with the funeral director. I enter the place of worship, usually through a side door, and I take my seat on the platform or wherever I'll be sitting. When the funeral director appears at the door, I stand and ask the congregation to rise. Patiently, everyone waits as the family is escorted to their seats. Once the last member of the family is seated, I ask the attendees to also take their seats.

A funeral does not just happen on its own but is the result of a plan and a team of players. Songs, whether congregational or specials, have been carefully and prayerfully considered. The minister's message, poems or readings, and other speeches must be inserted in appropriate places by someone, usually the officiating minister. Thinking in terms of "blocks," I may begin with one block to include greetings, the obituary, and scripture reading. Then there may be a block of music, followed by a block to include the sermon and benediction.

Once the order of service is finalized, copies should be made and given to the funeral directors, sound technician, soloists, instrumentalists, and ministers. This is not the funeral folder that is provided to everyone by the funeral home. This is merely a slip of paper with the actual step-by-step outline of worship that is received by only those involved in the mechanics of the service. I've found that funeral directors are so appreciative of this. My practice is to type the order on my laptop, six to a page. I print one or two pages, cut them apart, and distribute them. Here are a couple sample orders of service:

JIMMY DAVIS

Memorial Service

March 24, 2006

Musical Prelude

Opening/Scripture—Danny Goddard

Personal Comments

Amy Bates

Nita West

Special Song

Message—Danny Goddard

Closing Song—Vince Gill CD

Benediction—Danny Goddard

Musical Postlude

This service was for a person with whom I was not acquainted. We held the service in the sanctuary of our church, and it was well attended by many local people.

The next sample is from my father-in-law's service, which also took place in our sanctuary. While chatting with funeral director Tim Adams prior to the service, I pointed out Tom's usual seat, which was on the back row against the wall. I came back through the worship center a few moments later and saw that a red rose had been placed on that seat, a gesture that was very touching to everyone who took notice.

We had asked our worship leader to put together songs that Tom had enjoyed. Instrumentalists included our son, Tommy, the deceased's namesake and only grandchild. The result was a wonderful Spirit-filled and Spirit-led service in which a great man was honored and his Savior was worshipped and praised. Though not easy, I considered it an honor and privilege to preach Tom Waldrep's funeral. The order of service looked like this:

THOMAS ERWIN WALDREP
Friday, May 5, 2006

Organ Prelude	Bob Jung
Welcome, Obituary, Prayer	Rev. Kent Mullens
Worship and Praise	Reggie Coleman
Scripture	Rev. Joshua Lindley
Solo	Cindy Powell

"The Love of God"

Message	Rev. Danny Goddard

"Tom"

2 Timothy 4:7

Benediction	Dr. Carl Summer
Organ Postlude	Bob Jung

For the scripture reading, I like to put together a collection of passages to be read straight through without giving the references. I usually preface the readings with a brief statement about finding comfort in the Word of God. The passages are then read slowly and deliberately, allowing God's Holy Word to speak for itself.

3. **When?** The minister, the family of the deceased, and the funeral director all work together in finding a suitable time for the service. In biblical times, due to the hot climate of Palestine and surrounding areas, as well as poor embalming practices, a body was usually buried on the same day of death. Today's funeral service in America normally takes place three or four days after a person's

passing. This allows time for arrangements to be made at the funeral home by the family, the preparation of the body, and the visitation by family and friends, especially those from out of town. I once saw a body kept on display for over a week as the family was hopeful that certain relatives would be able to travel from a distance. It was obvious, however, that the funeral director, who was having to do daily touch-ups with makeup, was becoming more nervous with each passing day.

A family may think 10 A.M. on Tuesday morning would be a good time for the funeral, but when they check with the funeral director, they may discover that the funeral home already has a service scheduled at that time. If one of the services is in a different location, there might be no problem, unless the mortuary is small and lacks personnel. There is also a church calendar to consider. For example, it would not be wise to schedule a funeral service at the church if a denominational regional meeting is taking place nearby involving that local congregation. Usually a family will understand these kinds of circumstances and will try to find a time that is best for everyone.

4. Where? As mentioned earlier, if you are a pastor or a staff person, as you meet with the family of the deceased, you should offer the use of your church facilities. Again, the church calendar should be respected. For example, if a megachurch is fully decorated for their big-time annual Christmas event, it may be best to find another location for the memorial. Such church productions may take days, if not weeks, to break down and reconstruct sets, making other special services such as funerals not impossible, but improbable. It would be considerate of a family to understand. Should a family have no ties with any particular house of worship, almost every funeral home has a chapel that provides a sacred setting for such services. Either way, those involved need to make a decision about the place of tribute, and here the minister can be a tremendous help.

In our ever-changing nomadic world, we find so many people living in one town or state with their roots elsewhere. Many times families are torn between having the funeral here or there. If a person who has died did not live in a particular city for a long time and if he or she did not have a huge following of friends or family in that place, it is reasonable to have the service "back home." That's where the crowd will gather. Any sympathizers in the first town could drop by at a formal visitation to pay their respects the day before the body is taken from Oklahoma to Georgia or from whatever place to wherever. In the event the departed lived in a town for ten or twenty years and had a great host of friends, it would be fitting to have a funeral in both places. Sometimes families choose to have a funeral in the city where Dad died, then have a graveside service in the old country church two states away. A family's pocketbook is a big consideration, as well, and only they know what they can afford.

Clearly, much thinking goes into the "where" of the funeral service. Once the family, funeral director, and clergy have all agreed on a time and place, then plans can move ahead.

5. **Why?** I think the key word here is "closure." A family really needs to go through a traditional rite or ceremony to complete this part of life. For those two or three days of visitation, family members are being greeted by relatives and friends. Once you come to the funeral, you've come to the moment that makes all things final. This is where the "comma" is replaced by the "period" to a person's life in order for other lives to continue. We never forget that person we loved so dearly, but life goes on. We allow him or her to continue to live in our hearts and minds through so many dear and precious memories, yet we must continue on. My parents have been gone for over thirty years, yet there is not a week that goes by without my thinking of them several times. It's that funeral or memorial service that helps close the door to one chapter of our lives in order to introduce one that's new.

A man in my church became very ill and traveled to a large metropolitan city in another state for surgery and treatment. It was there, only days after major surgery, that he suddenly passed away. Realizing the seriousness of his situation before leaving town, he spoke with me and had been very adamant about having no funeral, and naturally, his widow and daughter wanted to honor his wishes. I phoned a pastor friend in that city and asked him to visit the grieving twosome for me. He did so and told me later that he asked them pertinent questions and had them share some great memories. In essence, he walked them through a "funeral" for their loving husband and father without their awareness. They needed the closure.

Once the funeral service has ended, the minister usually moves to the casket and stands at the head. The funeral directors approach the casket, open it (if there is to be a final viewing), and instruct people on how to file by for a last glance. As they pass, most people shake the minister's hand and offer some form of a thank-you. Some ignore you. Others have no clue as to what to do. It's OK. After all the friends have completed their viewing, the sanctuary doors are usually closed to allow the family some moments of privacy. Relatives are brought by the casket and led back to their seats. After the family is comfortable with their final good-byes, the pastor typically leads in prayer, praying for the Comforter to strengthen these good people. As he or she prays, the funeral directors will take the opportunity of bowed heads and closed eyes to close and lock the casket for the last time, a sight that no family member wants to see. Again, the procedure of these last moments may vary among mortuaries and funeral directors.

Many years ago, a wiser and older pastor friend told me that "once the funeral begins, the pastor never leaves the body." I have always remembered that. When the coffin is sealed and the family is ready, the minister leads the way out of the chapel or church to the waiting coach. The preacher stands by the rear of the hearse as pallbearers carefully place the casket inside. Once the rear door is closed, the minister goes to the vehicle that he or she will take to the cemetery. The funeral is now history, but we're not done yet.

7
WHAT SHALL I SAY?

"Moses My servant is dead. Now therefore, arise, go
over this Jordan, you and all this people, to the land
which I am giving to them—the children of Israel. . . .
No man shall be able to stand before you all the days
of your life; as I was with Moses, so I will be with you"
(Josh. 1:2, 5).

Although he was not granted the privilege of escorting them into
the Promised Land, Moses had been the chosen one of God to lead
the Israelites out of Egyptian bondage. Then he died. It was the
end of an era. Gone was a great leader. Moses had made speech after speech to Pharaoh, and finally, after a series of terrible plagues
upon the people, he persuaded the Egyptian king to release his
slaves. Even then, after the deed was done, the fickle leader of
Egypt changed his mind, perhaps initiating the first recorded high-
speed chase with horses and chariots.

At the climax of an exciting pursuit that backed the Israelites
up against the Red Sea, Moses raised the rod of God, parting the
waters in two walls on the left and the right. With the spray of mist
in their faces, he led the redeemed across on dry ground. Later to
provide for the need of his people, Moses used the rod of God to

bring clear water from a hard rock and meals of manna from the skies. He descended from Mount Sinai with the commandments of God finger-engraved on a tablet of stone. All of these tremendous feats had their beginning in a talking, perpetually burning bush in the middle of some pastureland. Now Moses was gone, and it was so very hard for everyone to believe.

As we read the first chapter of Joshua, it's almost as if God is preaching Moses' memorial message:

Moses My servant is dead. Now therefore, arise. . . . [The leader has departed, so it's now time for Joshua to get up and get going.] Every place that the sole of your foot will tread upon I have given you, as I said to Moses. . . . [God is reminding Joshua of how He had directed and protected Moses in the past and that He can do the same for him.] as I was with Moses, so I will be with you. . . . [He was promising His presence for Joshua in the same way that He had accompanied Moses.] be strong and very courageous, that you may observe to do according to all the law which Moses My servant commanded you. . . . Remember the word which Moses the servant of the LORD commanded you. . . . [In these lines, God reminds Joshua of the unswerving leadership of Moses and his instructions concerning obedience to the law of God.] you shall return to the land of your possession and enjoy it, which Moses the LORD's servant gave you on this side of the Jordan. . . . [God wants Joshua to realize that through Moses He had made the portion of land possible.] Just as we heeded Moses in all things, so we will heed you. Only the LORD your God be with you, as He was with Moses [Again, here is a powerful reminder that God had never left Moses and He would also never leave Joshua.] (vv. 2-5, 7, 13, 15, 17).

It's as if God is eulogizing Israel's former chief, preaching his funeral, so to speak. He's pointing out to Joshua all the positive features of Moses' life and leadership. By explaining His friendship with and faithfulness to former management, God is making promises and giving assurances to one who faces a most difficult task, that of leading the Israelites into Canaan Land. In short, the Creator of the universe is offering Joshua hope in the shadow of a fallen hero. These are the kinds of words that are spoken by either a minister or a layperson as he or she officiates at a funeral or memorial service.

1. Words of comfort. Dr. Robert Anderson firmly believes the funeral is the time to "bring words of comfort and hope to people who are hurting."[1] The place to begin this process is always with God's Word. The Bible is like no other book. It's not magic, but it is inspired and should be read different from any other work. It is the anointed Word of God, and when it is read silently or aloud, the Holy Spirit speaks loud and clear.

My maternal grandmother became a Christian in her seventies. I was privileged to stand at the altar with her when she was officially received into the membership of the church. On her first Christmas as a born-again believer, Sandie and I gave her the gift of a new Bible—a *New International Version.* We thought she could understand an NIV better than some other translations, but we did not realize that she failed to comprehend this whole "Word of God thing." She is to be commended for reading that Bible straight through, from cover to cover, something that many believers have never done. However, once the goal had been achieved, she commented over the telephone, "I finished reading that book you gave me. Now I need to find another book to read!" In her mind, she had read her "book," her Bible, once, so why read it again? From that point until the day she died, our annual Christmas gift for my grandmother was a different translation or paraphrase of God's Holy Word to keep her reading the Scriptures.

This is a good place to acknowledge that the Bible does not *contain* the Word of God—it *is* the Word of God. Sixty-six books have been inspired by the Holy Spirit, authoritative words written by the pens or quills of doctors, shepherds, kings, queens, tax collectors, tentmakers, fishermen, and those from other walks of life. Some of those books were penned centuries apart, and yet throughout the pages of both Old and New Testaments there runs the scarlet thread of Christ's blood, which makes all the difference in the world.

Sinners can read these God-inspired words and find salvation. Believers can dig into the Sacred Scriptures and find the way to a rewarding life of second-blessing holiness. And heartbroken mourners can certainly ponder the powerful words in the Holy Book to find comfort and hope in a time of loss. Marva Dawn writes, "Everybody is hunting for hope."[2] This hope is at hand, oozing from and around the words of Scripture. It's really found nowhere else.

When delivering the funeral message, you'll want to take a text and preach from God's Word, but even if your part is only a five-minute eulogy, why not base your thoughts around a verse from the Bible? You can never go wrong with presenting His Word, for it is such an encouraging resource of tremendous comfort. It has a power that will continue to speak to the hearts of the listeners for weeks, months, perhaps even years to come. The prophet believed God's Word would never "return . . . void" (Isa. 55:11), for again, it's like no other book. "For the word of God is living and powerful, and sharper than any two-edged sword" (Heb. 4:12).

There was not a more secluded place in the world than the Isle of Patmos, a barren rock out in the middle of the sea. This was the site where John was left alone. The apostle had been exiled to that prison island as punishment for simply following Jesus. He sat there all by himself, day in and day out. And then to make matters worse, Sunday was coming! There would be no choir to sing the beautiful hymns of the church, no praise team to lead the congregation in worship, no PowerPoint slide show to help in note taking, no preacher to eloquently deliver the message of God, not even a congregation to join with John in lifting the name of Jesus. It was just John on a jagged rock. But even in such a dismal and depressing setting, look at the apostle's affirmation: "I was in the Spirit on the Lord's Day" (Rev. 1:10). The disciple whom Jesus loved didn't need all of those other things to be content. All he required was the Divine Presence, for He alone brings comfort. Yes, a funeral is a sad and somber occasion, but it is also a time when we can find comfort in the powerful Word of God.

2. **Words of compliment.** As I tried to stress in a previous chapter, a funeral is *for* the ones who have been left behind, but it is *about* the one who has passed on. While there certainly are many other components to such services, the primary purpose of the gathering is to remember the deceased. If there is ever a time to compliment a person on his or her life, here it is.

I attended an evening memorial service that paid fitting tribute to a former professor at one of our Nazarene universities. The service lasted over an hour and included several passages from the Bible, extremely kind words from the pastor, at least four uplifting eulogies from close friends, a musical compliment played on the organ, and the singing of three or four hymns that had been arranged by the deceased himself. Though he and I had never crossed paths, I left that church feeling as though I had known that professor.

That's what funerals are supposed to do—eulogize, honor, pay tribute to the one who had lived. Our words and thoughts should make him or her "live" once again, at least for thirty minutes in the hearts of those gathered together. This would be a great opportunity to remember some of the person's attributes, talents, accomplishments. What kind of person was he or she? What were some of his or her finest traits? What kinds of complimentary things did others say about the departed? Tell some stories and even draw laughter from a congregation of grievers.

You may have heard the story about the lady who sat at her husband's funeral. The minister had so many complimentary things to say about her spouse—what a wonderful man he had been, how he had influenced the lives of so many. On and on he went, using adjectives that dripped with honey, presenting such a positive picture of the deceased. Finally, the widow stood and looked into the casket. The funeral director asked if there was a problem, to which she replied, "Oh no. I just wanted to make sure I was at the right service!" By no means am I suggesting the message and eulogies should be far-fetched, but with a little time and effort, I think we can find some positive things to say about everyone.

3. **Words of commitment.** Every memorial message should come to a point of commitment. If we are satisfied with the spiritual condition of our departed brother or sister, then sound it from the rooftop! Let it be known that Cousin LeNora had made her peace with God and even relate the story (if you know it) of how God gloriously saved her soul. There will always be a loved one or a friend present who does not know Jesus as Savior. That person needs to hear this story!

What if you are not sure about the person's spiritual life (or lack thereof)? What if you cannot feel comfortable about his or her soul's present whereabouts? Perhaps you knew this person lived a godless life and you could almost say for certain that he or she missed it! Notice I said "almost" say that he or she missed it. This is something that no one ever knows for sure. We'll never know what might have gone through a person's mind in those final, fleeting seconds prior to death. We'll never know whether or not she breathed a quick prayer of repentance before the car crashed. We'll never know if he had opportunity to repent just before that fatal heart attack. We just don't know! So how can we condemn a person's soul to an undesirable place when we have no way of being certain?

In light of this kind of thinking, let's present a merciful God of grace who is the righteous Judge and commit the departed soul to Him. We don't preach the deceased into heaven nor do we condemn a soul to hell. We merely point people to Jesus. We use the Word to show the kind of life that is expected of us in order to guarantee the future of an unbroken circle. Stan Toler offers guidelines on delivering the funeral message: "Make it scriptural, brief (ten to fifteen minutes), personal, and clear without being preachy (incorporate the salvation plan)."[3]

If you volunteer your services at a local mortuary and the staff starts calling you to officiate at funerals for families that have neither church nor pastor, chances are you'll be preaching over the bodies of some lost souls. Just remember it is not up to us to determine whether or not a person was a Christian. We can still offer words of comfort and read passages of Scripture that will uplift and encourage anyone who's rough around the edges. We can still present words of compliment, for regardless of spirituality, everyone knows he was a great grandpa, without question she loved her kids, and it was public knowledge that he would have given you the shirt off his back. We can still say words of commitment and allow God to be God. I have laid to rest many individuals whose souls I have had to commit to the Lord and leave in His hands.

So we prayerfully prepare a message and show up at the service with our manuscript or outline, whatever we're preaching from. We have carefully weighed every word, fully believing these thoughts came directly from the heart of God. We are now ready to proclaim the Word, eulogize someone who deserves some credit, and try to help some grieving folk along the way. We have the plan. But then sometimes our plan goes straight out the window.

Bonnie was a first-time visitor at our services on a Sunday morning. About Tuesday of that next week, she phoned me at the church. After identifying herself, I told her that I did remember meeting her and that we were thrilled to have her in church. She called to ask a favor: Would I be willing to preach her husband's graveside service on Thursday morning? Immediately, I felt such sorrow for her. "I'm so sorry," I exclaimed. "When did your husband pass away?" Since all seemed to be well on Sunday morning, I assumed this must have happened either later Sunday or sometime on Monday, perhaps late Monday evening. Bonnie's answer stunned me: "About two years ago!"

As briefly as she could, she told me her story. A few years ago Bonnie and her husband purchased some spaces in a local cemetery. The plots were located in a new area that was under construction. The graves in this section were double-decker graves! By that I mean that two caskets would be buried in the same plot, one over the other. The first to expire would be laid to rest on the bottom, a slab would go overhead, and the grave would then be covered with dirt. Months or years later, when the widow or widower passes away, the grave is reopened and the remaining casket is laid on top of the slab, and the grave is closed a second and final time. When this couple purchased these spaces, they were told that the site would not be finished for a couple of years. In the meantime, the untimely death of Earl was a surprise to everyone. They had a funeral for him after which his casket was temporarily entombed in a mausoleum. My new friend explained that the cemetery had just called to say the construction was finally complete and the remains of her loved one would be properly buried on Thursday.

Of course, I agreed to do the service. Prayerfully searching my Bible, I landed on John 14, that powerful and personal passage where Jesus breaks the news to His disciples that He was going away to prepare a place for them for eternity. It was just before ten o'clock on a beautiful sunny Thursday when Sandie and I met a handful of people at the mausoleum. I can't remember if the temporary tomb was on the second or third floor of this huge crypt, but I do recall climbing stairs. We followed Bonnie down the corridor until she froze in her tracks. We looked up in the direction she was looking. About seven places up was an open burial chamber. The widow became extremely agitated. The body appeared to have already been removed, and yet she had been under the impression that nothing would be done until the immediate family had arrived. "I saw him go in," she exclaimed, "and I wanted to see him come out!"

Demanding to see the manager of the cemetery, our friend was escorted to a foyer area in the mausoleum. We followed. A few minutes later, a very diplomatic woman appeared and informed us that the manager was unavailable but that she could help us with any problem. The dilemma was presented. The manager's representative shuffled through some papers and admitted that there had been a communication mishap. We all were under the impression that we were going to have a short service in the chapel of the mausoleum, but the cemetery workers had orders for a direct burial. The gravediggers were innocently unaware that there was to be an audience.

After the widow and her upset family calmed down, Bonnie inquired about the whereabouts of her husband's body. The lady in charge pointed out a side window. We all looked and saw a pine casket, about chest-high, dangling from chains on a backhoe! The widow asked how she could know that was her husband. We were led out the door and down the steps to the hanging coffin. The lady showed us a small plaque at one end of the pine box that bore Earl's full name. They were obviously not expecting visitors that morning, for the dust on that casket was thick enough for you to write his name with your finger directly on the wood.

The cemetery lady apologized profusely and then informed her employees that we were there to have a service. The chapel, however, was far from being ready. I think they had some pews stacked up, which left it in a state of disarray. Besides, the casket was already on the backhoe! The decision was finally made to have a short service at the grave itself.

We all got into our cars and lined up in a procession with my car being the lead. On second thought, I'll take that back. The backhoe was the lead. Very slowly, the five or six cars followed behind Sandie and me as we followed the tractor, the almost hypnotic casket swinging by a chain from side to side in front of us. My wife and I said nothing to each other. We were both dumbfounded. This had to have been one of the most awkward moments in our ministry.

We arrived at a stark opening in the ground. There was no mechanical apparatus outlining the grave that would slowly lower the coffin into its final resting place. There was no artificial turf to disguise the loose brown dirt. There were neither folding chairs set up nor a tent for overhead. It was just a naked hole in the ground. The tractor was positioned until the casket hung over the open grave, and then the cemetery personnel backed away, removed their hard hats, and patiently waited. I heard the sobs of a few family members. This time, I don't think the tears were as much for the loss of someone who had been gone for twenty-some months as they were for the lack of dignity in the entire comedy of errors. I stepped up as close to the casket as I could, for there evidently had been a leak in the seal. I took my little sermon outline that I had prayerfully and painstakingly written, and I tucked it away in the back of my Bible. It just didn't seem to fit anymore. My plan no longer agreed with the circumstances.

Turning to John's Gospel, chapter 14, I began, "Let not your heart be troubled . . ." The scripture was the text I had planned, but the message came out completely different. I just said aloud that things had not happened the way anyone had anticipated for that day. I then introduced the disciples of John 14, explaining that they were confused and frightened, for Jesus was breaking the news that He was going away. The Holy Spirit very definitely directed me that morning as I delivered one of those impromptu messages that always seem to be the best.

I prayed, and we stepped away and stood by our cars. When the cemetery people saw that no one was leaving, they very carefully began their work, slowly lowering one end of the coffin into the hole by the chain. With the casket not far from a vertical position, the one end finally touched bottom and the entire case could then be lowered into the ground. The relief on the faces of the gravediggers was noticeable. I was later secretly told that they really did not think there was enough chain but they certainly didn't want to drop Earl in front of his family!

There will, no doubt, be such occasions when a preacher will not be able to deliver a textbook sermon but will instead end up preaching off-the-cuff. In those moments, and thank God they're not often, all we have to rely upon is the blessed Holy Spirit. What shall we say? We say whatever He lays on our hearts.

8
TRADITION

"Jesus replied, 'Let her alone. She did it in preparation
for my burial'" (John 12:7, TLB).

Tradition. In Jesus' day, it was traditional to anoint a body with fragrant perfumes and spices, the only embalming practice people knew. This was the intention of Mary, the sister of Lazarus, who shocked everyone at a dinner in Bethany by pouring expensive spikenard over the head of Jesus. He even explained that her actions were merely to prepare His body for entombment. Tradition. Whenever I think of tradition, I feel like heartily breaking out in that powerful song titled in its honor from *Fiddler on the Roof*— except I don't know all the words. So abandoning that idea, I'll just share a few things about tradition as it relates to today's funeral industry. Because of the diversity of regions, cultures, and even practices among funeral directors, traditions throughout the nation and even around the world differ greatly.

I lectured in Professor Vicki Copp's Theology of Church and Ministry class at Nazarene Theological Seminary in Kansas City. For an hour I gave a presentation, titled "Ministry in the Mourning," that explained how to pastor those who are dying and then officiate at the funeral and do all the rest that follows. At the end of the class, ten minutes or so remained for questions, and the first came from a young ministerial student concerning tradition. In moving from one part of the United States to another, he had noticed some variation with funerals and committals and wondered if the location had anything to do with the contrasts he had observed. The answer to his question was undoubtedly yes! Let's see how tradition influences the funeral industry.

1. **Tradition with flowers**. In the Deep South, sending beautiful sprays of flowers for a funeral or memorial service has always been important. Most Southern funeral homes have permanent hooks on the walls of their chapels and slumber rooms for colorful sprays to be attached. They also have portable stands that will hold spray arrangements when they are to be moved to and from one locale to another. I would speculate that most of the flowers seen at a funeral in the South would be in the form of sprays.

Sandie and I moved from North Carolina to our second pastorate, a small church in the state of Nebraska. There are lots of differences between the Carolinas and Nebraska: tall trees as opposed to the lack thereof; red dirt versus black soil; and, oh yes, a difference in accent. Growing up three exits from downtown Atlanta, I had always had a deep Southern drawl, so much so that my wife had to interpret for me at our new bank and in grocery stores. And everyone always followed up our conversations with, "I just love to hear people speak with a Southern accent!" After hearing this a few times, my usual reply became, "If you'll come to Columbus Church of the Nazarene, you can hear thirty minutes of it every Sunday morning!"

Shortly after our cross-country move, I had to call a local florist to order some funeral flowers. Because of my upbringing, I naturally tried to order a spray of flowers, but the florist politely informed me that people in the Midwest do not normally send sprays. Their practice is to send potted flowers. At first I didn't want to send flowers in a pot—I wanted them in a spray. We discussed this for several minutes, and I finally accepted her advice. We loved our five years in Nebraska, and while there, I don't think I ever saw a single spray at a funeral. There was absolutely nothing wrong with that. It was just, for me, different. Tradition.

2. **Tradition with funeral directors.** Although I would guess that most undertakers have the same academic degree, I have discovered that they may not always do everything the same. For example, in the procession from the service to the cemetery, not all funeral directors arrange the cars in the same order. Some directors start with the funeral coach, followed by the minister's vehicle, then the family car. Others put the family ahead of the minister. Still others have family cars in front of the hearse. This practice is not even a geographical matter, for I've seen such differences among mortuaries within the same city. Apparently, there is no chart hanging at the school of mortuary science to diagram the proper processional lineup.

Some morticians prefer that the pallbearers wear boutonnieres on their lapels, while others don't. I remember that at the conclusion of the committal for my mother-in-law, the funeral director had a little ritual he liked to do. As a final act of tribute and respect, he instructed the pallbearers to file by the grave site, remove their flowers, and place them on top of the casket. I also vaguely remember witnessing this in some other place. One by one they obeyed, and then came pallbearer number six. He was our cousin, a big, tall, rather intimidating fellow who said to the undertaker in a loud, boisterous voice, "That's my aunt and this flower's staying right here!" Though the family knows he's completely harmless, no one from the funeral profession argued with him.

I once observed a practice at a Midwestern mortuary that I had never seen before nor have I seen since. Upon my arrival at the funeral, I noticed that cars had been deliberately parked extremely close to the rear of the coach, so close that I remember thinking, *Someone has messed up here. They're not going to be able to get that rear door open.* When the service was over and we came out with the casket, I watched with interest to see what was going to happen. The six pallbearers carried the coffin to the waiting coach. To my surprise, the funeral director opened a side door near the rear of the hearse, slid the casket onto some kind of a sleeve that was on a pivot, turned it slightly to line it up straight, and closed the door! Over the years I noticed that this was the way that particular funeral home did it every time I attended a service there. Sandie and I used to tease each other that when it was our time to go, we want to go in through the back door as you're supposed to, not the side! Tradition!

3. **Tradition with caskets.** You would think that all caskets and coffins pretty much look alike. There are the steel ones and the wooden ones. There are caskets that seem masculine, while others have more of a feminine look. You can purchase coffins in various gauges of steel, and you can get ones that seal and others that don't. And you can find them with themes: cowboys or NASCAR or Harley-Davidson motorcycles or even college football teams. All kinds of things from trees and wildlife to praying hands and religious symbols can be found adorning the lining. Though some of the themes or graphics may be regional, available styles of caskets are similar just about everywhere.

A funeral director did show me something interesting once in caskets. I had grown up around caskets that had lids divided in half. The bottom half remains closed, hiding the body from the waist down, while the upper half is opened for viewing the deceased from the waist up. Looking through a catalog picturing various caskets and coffins for purchase, I came across one without a divided lid. The lid was one piece that covered the length of the casket. This means that when it is opened for viewing, the body can be seen from head to toe. Having not seen one like that, I questioned the undertaker, who explained that the one-lid casket was popular in another section of the United States. I heard the other day about a casket that "breaks down," leaving the departed one out in the open on a display pedestal.

4. **Tradition with people.** We all know that when it's all said and done, people are just people, yet funeral and burial practices can differ, especially between people groups. I don't pretend to be an expert on every people group and what they do or do not do at a time of death, but I am familiar with a few. As mentioned earlier, I participated once in a Samoan funeral held in our church on the coast of North Carolina. What a beautiful and meaningful service it was. The music was nothing short of heavenly, with a beautiful South Seas sound. When making the arrangements, the family requested many things—from speakers and singers to special rituals—and they wanted all presentations except for mine to be made in their native tongue. Rather than guess when all of their rites and rituals were done, I just told the family to observe their usual traditions and then nod when it was my turn.

I recall another occasion while attending Trevecca Nazarene University in Nashville. I drove by an African-American church one Friday night and noticed that its parking lot was full and that cars also had lined the street. Immediately I was curious about what was attracting the crowd. Then I spotted a hearse parked in front of the steps, an unusual sight on a Friday night. Since it was a warm spring evening, the front doors of the church were opened wide and the sanctuary was all lit up. As I slowly drove by, I saw people inside the little church clad in bright colored robes and dancing down the center aisle. It so intrigued me that I circled the block for another look! They were obviously having a wake for some departed soul.

A former missionary in our local church told me about conducting a funeral once for someone in Africa. He said that at the conclusion of the service they set fire to a pyre and burned the body right there on the spot. Tradition.

5. **Tradition with visitation.** Visiting a mortuary and viewing the body of a friend or loved one is an important part of closure. Years ago, the body was brought to the residence and mourners and well-wishers would stop by the house to visit with the family. Eventually, funeral parlors took on a homey look and became known as funeral *homes*. The hope is that people can find in these places an atmosphere that is quiet, calming, and comforting during the time of death. Usually there are comfortable chairs and couches and even quiet music playing in the background. Everything says, "Come on in and stay awhile." A viewing at a mortuary is not to be a rushed act.

We live in a busy time where everyone is rushing here and there. It's the day of cell phones, microwave ovens, and one-hour services. I suppose that's the reason a particular funeral home in South Carolina began holding drive-by viewings! My district superintendent in Southwest Oklahoma, Dr. Carl Summer, read about it in a newspaper and he called the funeral home on the telephone to verify the facts. It was all true. On your way home from work, you can whip into the parking lot of the funeral home, drive past the viewing window as if you were making a deposit at a bank or ordering fries through a speaker, see how "nice" the departed looks, and drive back out to the street. The entire experience is over perhaps before the traffic light changes on the corner! I guess if I were the one placed on display in the window, I would prefer speed bumps be set in place to at least slow down my mourners a bit as they drive by for their final good-bye.

I grew up in Atlanta, where formal visitations were not scheduled at the local funeral homes. When a loved one was lying in state, the family camped out right there at the funeral parlor until the body was buried. Although the business would close at a decent hour at night and not allow anyone else to enter, we were told that we could take our time and leave when we were ready to do so. At the age of nineteen, I spent almost two complete days and evenings in the state room with the remains of my mom. Relatives and friends tried to entice me to leave for a while to go to a restaurant or somewhere else, but I felt obligated to stay right there, as did my brother and sister, Harold and Vickie. I think we were there when they opened around 8 A.M., and we stayed till shortly after closing, around 9 P.M. A few years later, I moved to another state and discovered that in some places you have only two hours of visitation, 7 P.M. to 9 P.M., and that seemed so odd to me.

Prior to being elected general superintendent in the Church of the Nazarene, Dr. Jim Diehl pastored some strong churches, one of them being my home church, Atlanta First. It was the late seventies and Dr. Diehl had just recently become our pastor. My call to ministry was not even yet a year old. Taking a personal interest in me, Pastor Diehl became my lifelong mentor. Many times whenever I was home from college for a holiday break, my pastor would take me calling with him. As we drove across the city, we wasted no time. He would say, "Today let's talk about how to give an altar call." Pastor Diehl would talk, and I would take notes (which I still have in a file to this day).

Sandie and I were dating at that time, and I remember that we had come home from school for the Thanksgiving-Christmas break. She spent those few weeks working in the church office. It was the day after Thanksgiving and no one was around. Since Sandie was the only one working in the office that day, I went along with her for company. On those rare occasions when I was in town and Pastor Diehl was away, he would let me sit in his study and look at his commentaries. Sandie still calls it "pretending to be a pastor," but whatever you wish to call it, that's what I was doing.

It was on that holiday Friday when Sandie received "the phone call." A man had passed away. I recognized his name from the weekly prayer list but did not know him. He was one of those people who never came to church but was "associated" somehow with the congregation. Sandie immediately tracked down Pastor Diehl at the home of friends in South Georgia, where he and his family had spent Thanksgiving. He was going to be heading back soon, but the distance between Wrightsville and Atlanta would make it impossible to be back in order to visit the family that day. Knowing how eager I was to do some "pastoring," Rev. Diehl got me on the phone and asked me to represent him by dropping by the funeral home to call on the family. Within minutes, I was on I-40 heading for downtown Atlanta, where the old historic mortuary was located.

I had never been to this particular funeral home. It wasn't your typical brick building but was rather an old mansion, two, perhaps three, stories tall, not far from the Fulton County Stadium, where the Braves played. A bell chimed on my entering the front door, but no one was there to greet me. I walked a few steps into the creaky old house and saw framed photographs everywhere— different sizes and of different people, individual shots and family portraits, hanging on walls and standing on tables. A man suddenly appeared from a back room wearing a white shirt, a tie, and black pants. He inquired of my presence, and I explained my reason for being there. He informed me that the family had not yet arrived, but he pointed to the room of the deceased, saying that I could wait for them there. I thanked him and he vanished as quickly as he had appeared.

Stepping up a level, I went into the room that had been pointed out. It was dark and long. Since it was the '70s and I was wearing platform shoes, my heels were too loud on the hardwood floor, so I slowed my pace and almost tiptoed. The casket was located at the far end of the room, nestled between two tall lamps with glass globes that gave off a pink hue. Except for a few lamps on tables along the walls, those two lamps were the only source of light. I approached the casket and looked at the deceased, not recognizing him. Noticing the Masonic apron around his waist, I began to study some of the symbols that it displayed.

Suddenly, I heard a faint noise, a clicking or smacking sound. Thinking the family had arrived, I looked around but saw no one. I listened in the quiet, and a minute or so later I heard it again. The sound seemed to be coming from the head of the casket, so I took a few steps toward that end and leaned down close to the face of the departed. Only seconds later, I heard the sound again, most definitely from the area of his lips, and all of a sudden one corner of his mouth came open!

Understandably startled, I jumped back, quickly concluding that the family was not going to show that afternoon, and I left in a hurry. It must have been the loud sound of my shoes on the wooden floor that brought the funeral director back out from his work. Running into him in the foyer, I told him I needed to leave but that whatever was keeping that body's lips together was losing its hold! He pulled something out of his pocket that looked like ChapStick and headed one direction while I went the other. When I related this episode to my later-to-be mother-in-law, Juanita, she responded, "The first time he started smacking, I would have gone smackin' right out of there!"

Although we were in the Deep South where many families keep vigil by their loved ones, here was a family that had evidently broken the tradition of camping out at the local mortuary. They had obviously opted to come and go, but I failed to wait long enough to meet them. I did leave word with the funeral home personnel to pass along the message that I had been there. Tradition.

6. **Tradition with cemeteries.** You guessed it. Burial places are not all the same either. There are church graveyards in rural settings, and there are perpetual-care memorial gardens in the city,

with lots of rules and regulations. Some burial grounds have tombstones of differing heights, while others only allow flat markers that make it easy to mow. Some cemeteries allow committals to take place under a canvas at the grave site, while others require the committal to be done inside a mausoleum chapel, with the burial taking place after everyone has gone. And then there's winter. In several of the northern states the ground is frozen for several months of the year and all the bodies are stored someplace until spring. Families then receive some sort of notice by mail informing them of the burial of their loved ones. Tradition.

Why did I write an entire chapter about tradition? It's because tradition is a very important part of life. It is who we are and where we're from. Tradition is what makes each of us unique from one another. Tradition is the thing that also makes us just like each other.

Tradition is something that must be respected by ministers of all kinds. Who cares if the lid on the casket is made up of one, two, or three parts? What does it matter if the flowers are in a pot or fanned out as a spray? And what if the family sits by the deceased from morning until night or just drops by occasionally throughout the day or races by the drive-up window or perhaps doesn't visit at all? Traditions may be different, but people are still the same. They still hurt and sob and ache from the feeling that their loved one has been ripped from them. They still are reaching for a word of encouragement, an assurance that someone can make sense of all of this. They need the ministry that only their pastor or caregiver or best friend can give. Whatever their tradition may be, the bereaved are in the perfect state to hear the voice of God. Professor Richard Stoll Armstrong helps us here:

> People are never more receptive to what is said from the pulpit than they are at a funeral. Some are longing for a word of hope or comfort. Some are searching for answers to agonizing questions. Some are seeking to fill the huge void in their lives

from the loss of a loved one or close friend. Some are eager to hear the reassuring message of the resurrection to eternal life. Whatever their need at the moment, they are as ready as they have ever been to hear the word of the Lord.[1]

I sat in the balcony of Nashville First Church of the Nazarene on a Sunday morning. Dr. Millard Reed was the senior pastor and was ever so eloquently delivering a message of encouragement. God's Spirit was upon him as he was preaching to his congregation about the storms of life. If anyone could identify with his message that morning, it was I. Only two years had passed since I had lost my mom, and only a matter of months had gone by since I had lost my dad. The pain was still present. The hole in my heart was still real. Somewhere on my worship folder that morning, I scribbled a statement that Pastor Reed made, words that I have remembered for some thirty years: "There is always a ray of sunlight shining from the very face of Jesus."[2]

My dear minister friend, respect and honor the traditions of the families and the funeral homes. Remain flexible, realizing this funeral director may do it different from the one last month. Allow room for change in your own mind about flowers or caskets or even which door is the right door on the hearse. And above all, minister Christ to those with broken hearts.

9
THE PROCESSION

"It was a huge funeral procession" (Gen. 50:9, TM).

Pallbearers slid the silver casket into the back of the shiny black
funeral coach that was parked under the drive-through on the east
side of the brick mortuary. The undertaker, assuring me he would
return momentarily, disappeared along with the six men in dark
suits. I opened the passenger door to the coach, found my seat in
the front on the passenger side, closed the door, and waited . . . and
waited . . . and waited. The next thing I recall, I was waking up from
an impromptu nap! I am one of those who have been blessed with
the ability to slip into slumber whenever and wherever I become
relaxed, a skill that comes in handy on the bench at the mall, but
this time I had fallen asleep in a hearse! Glancing at my watch, I
was shocked to discover over thirty minutes had passed!

I frantically looked around and saw only the two police officers
who were still standing and chatting at the exit of the parking lot.
I whirled around and looked behind me. The floral-covered casket
was still in place. Feeling as if I were in the twilight zone, I opened
the door, left the funeral coach, and made my way to the front door
of the mortuary. Upon entering, I happily found all the people,

some standing, some sitting, and everyone visiting. The funeral director walked toward me, apologizing for not returning to the hearse as he had promised. He explained that a close relative of the deceased had taken ill and was lying down for a while in a lounge. Another fifteen minutes lapsed before she was assisted out to a waiting car. No one knew that I had been sawing logs in the hearse! We all took our places, and though slightly behind schedule, the procession to the cemetery began.

The journey to the final resting place is usually an emotionally difficult trip, one that no one wants to take, yet it is one that is inevitable. Usually, the deceased is accompanied by an entourage of friends and family members in support of the immediate family. This custom is not something that was dreamed up during the past century or two, but rather the concept is biblical. When Joseph went to bury the remains of his father, he did not make the trip alone, for a cast of characters went with him:

So Joseph went up to bury his father; and with him went up all the servants of Pharaoh, the elders of his house, and all the elders of the land of Egypt, as well as all the house of Joseph, his brothers, and his father's house. Only their little ones, their flocks, and their herds they left in the land of Goshen. And there went up with him both chariots and horsemen, and it was a very great gathering (Gen. 50:7-9).

Thousands of years have come and gone since those days, and so much has changed. We rarely use "chariots and horsemen," and we usually take longer to bury our dead. The practice of a funeral procession, however, remains.

The Procession

This ride to the place of interment or entombment, typically made with a string of cars and other vehicles, all moving at a snail's pace, is called the *procession*. A funeral procession has been properly defined as "an organized, dignified, solemn and respectful parade for the purpose of conveying the deceased and mourners from the place of service to the cemetery or crematorium for a committal service."[1]

Pastor David Busic preached a Sunday night sermon on death, taking his congregation back to the days of the Bible when the Romans referred to a burial place as the *necropolis*. Coming from a Greek word that means "death" or "dead," the word *necropolis* literally means "city of the dead." Because Christians looked forward to a future resurrection, they refuted the finality of death by replacing the term *necropolis* with *cemetery*, or "temporary place of rest." Through this modification they proclaimed that death did not have the last word![2]

Sometimes the procession is only a trip around the corner, for the departed may be buried in a nearby church graveyard. Other times, the grave is in a family plot a few miles across town. And in some cases, the interment may be an entire state away or perhaps farther. When the trip is going to take a matter of hours, the cars may leave separately but meet at a prearranged time at the place of burial.

The length of the procession always varies with each funeral. I've seen such a long row of cars, trucks, and SUVs that I was unable to find the last vehicle, a wonderful tribute to someone who had truly touched the lives of many people. I was not surprised when I heard that the procession for Princess Diana exceeded three and a half miles. More recently, I was part of a procession made up of only six vehicles, counting the funeral coach, the family limousine, and my car. A procession can even be smaller. I remember a funeral that a retired pastor friend officiated in Muncie, Indiana. The body had never been claimed, and the local newspaper ran a photograph taken during the memorial service. The picture showed the preacher delivering his message to only two men, who sat on the front row—the funeral directors! Most people don't spend much time thinking about the procession, but there are a few things that probably should be addressed.

The procession is always a topic of discussion when the arrangements are made at the funeral home. The director will ask about family cars. They will want to know whether limousines will be needed for the immediate family, and if so, how many? Some people at first don't see the need for limousines. Why go to such expense when you can drive yourself? But once you consider the peace of mind and lack of stress that comes with being driven to and from your loved one's final resting place, it's probably well worth the price. These long family cars are usually sent to the main residence to pick everyone up, and they will deliver the family back home at the end of the day. Often a limo is also secured to transport pallbearers. Again, it's the choice of the family.

I did see something at one funeral home in a northern state that I had never seen before. Parked in the parking lot was a huge camper-looking thing, somewhat similar to a recreational vehicle. This "funeral coach RV" replaced the hearse and family cars, transporting not only the casket but also six pallbearers and even the immediate family. It may be the way of the future.

Most funeral processions are treated with genuine respect, but sometimes there's a unique twist. Perhaps you heard the story of the funeral procession driving by the golf course where two golfers immediately ceased their playing and one of them even removed his hat and placed it over his heart. His friend was touched by his buddy's sensitivity, and he complimented him. His pal then replied, "It's the least I can do—we were married forty years next month!" Thankfully, that's a bit farfetched. Respectful motorists on both sides of the road usually come to a stop until the procession has completely passed. Some people standing along the way, such as construction workers or road crews, may remove their hats or place a hand over their hearts, a sight that is always comforting to mourners, especially to the next of kin.

A funeral procession is rarely intentionally stopped by anyone, for that would be a heartless and unthinkable act, yet that's exactly what happened one day near the city of Nain. Luke has recorded the scene:

And when He came near the gate of the city, behold, a dead man was being carried out, the only son of his mother; and she was a widow. And a large crowd from the city was with her. When the Lord saw her, He had compassion on her and said to her, "Do not weep." Then He came and touched the open coffin, and those who carried him stood still. And He said, "Young man, I say to you, arise." So he who was dead sat up and began to speak. And He presented him to his mother. Then fear came upon all, and they glorified God, saying, "A great prophet has risen up among us"; and, "God has visited His people." And this report about Him went throughout all Judea and all the surrounding region *(Luke 7:12-17)*.

The likes of that happening would still make news today, but seldom is there interference with a funeral entourage. As a matter of fact, in most places it is against the law to even break through a funeral procession.

My wife and I were following a coach in Wilmington, North Carolina, when a car failed to yield to our procession and very intentionally broke through the line. A police cruiser happened to be waiting at the traffic light, and as we approached the intersection, the funeral director driving the hearse caught the attention of the policeman and pointed to the motorist who had done the deed. The officer immediately turned on his blue beacons and sped away in the direction of the perpetrator. Most of the time, such incidents can be prevented if the cars stay close together. When huge gaps are left between vehicles, innocent drivers cannot always easily recognize what is taking place.

I have been in a few processions that did something out of the ordinary to show respect for the deceased. This first happened with the funerals for my parents. When my mom died, the First Church of the Nazarene was constructing its new building on Atlanta's south side, at I-285 near the Covington Highway exit. Since we could not have the funeral at the church (we had been holding services in a rented location), we opted for the chapel of the Horis A. Ward Funeral Home on Candler Road in Decatur. At the time I was not aware of the plan, but I did know the route to Georgia Memorial Park in Marietta, which was north of the city. Instead of heading out I-20 west to I-75 north at the downtown interchange, the procession headed out I-20 east, connecting with the bypass. It touched me deeply to realize we were taking my mother's body by the site of the new church that she would never attend.

When my dad passed away two years later, the church building had been constructed and he had enjoyed many services in that new facility. Harold, Vickie, and I decided, however, that we didn't want to do more for our dad than we had done for our mom, so we asked the undertaker to pull her file and duplicate it. Though the price had increased slightly, we had the same casket, the same vault, and the same funeral home chapel. And, oh yes, once again we made the trip around I-285, passing by the beautiful church building that my dad helped to erect.

Then there was a funeral held at a mortuary in Parker City, Indiana. The procession was taking us out of town to a rural setting where there was a little graveyard under a grove of trees. To get there, we would pass the old homestead on the farm of the deceased. Once we arrived at that point, the procession stopped on that country road and waited as the funeral coach drove into the gate and made a circle around the drive and out again. Many thoughtful comments were made later at the cemetery concerning that most meaningful drive-through.

The Privilege

Who may participate in the funeral procession? Anyone who desires. The lineup typically goes something like this: Most of the time, at least in the city, there is a police escort, either by car or motorcycle. In some cities, these are off-duty police officers who receive a small compensation on the side by making sure these processions make it safely to the memorial park. I have been part of processions that, when crossing a county line or leaving the city limits, an officer of a different jurisdiction was waiting to take over. This varies with different locations.

After the escort vehicle, there is usually the funeral coach or hearse. This is followed by the pastor's personal car, unless he or she is riding in the coach. I've done both. Then there are the limousines that transport the next of kin. The order of these vehicles is determined by the funeral director, and I've found them shuffled around in different orders from town to town, mortuary to mortuary.

After these lead vehicles, the procession is open to anyone: family members, friends, acquaintances, whoever wants to join in. Anyone and everyone is usually permitted and encouraged to accompany the deceased and his or her family to the grave site, unless the committal is to be private.

The Protocol

Driving in a funeral procession is not like driving to Wal-Mart. You must stay close to the car ahead of you so the line will not be broken. The entourage moves along and makes progress, but definitely at an unhurried speed. While riding in a hearse in Atlanta, I noticed the reminder in big bold letters that was taped to the Cadillac's dashboard: "Do Not Exceed 30 MPH." I suppose this snail's pace is done out of reverence for the departed. It just doesn't seem right to race to the graveyard. I also believe the deliberate crawl is to give the flower van a chance to arrive ahead of others. That way, upon entering the cemetery, everyone in the procession will see the beautiful floral arrangements all on display, the very same ones that had just graced the church sanctuary twenty minutes earlier.

For those driving in the official line, traffic lights and stop signs are ignored. This can be somewhat dangerous, especially when there is no police escort. I once took a college ministerial student with me to observe a funeral I officiated in Oklahoma. After leaving the funeral home, we approached the first intersection, prompting the police cruiser in front to sound his siren, bringing all traffic to a halt. Without touching a brake, we continued on, passing through the red light and making a left turn as the officer held back the cars. To my young friend who had never been in such a procession, running the red lights was the most exciting part of his day.

Some mortuaries provide magnetic flags that attach to the hood of your car as a way of identifying the procession. Others may put a bumper sticker-type sign in your front windshield. I suppose the most universal form of identification is your headlights. Each car in the entourage should burn headlights on high beam. This alerts other drivers even from a distance that there is something unusual about the oncoming traffic.

Hopefully, the procession will not be a stress test for those involved. A dear saint of the church passed away in one of our pastorates. He had told me once when I had visited with him, "Preacher, one day they're going to carry me into that church in a pine box and I want you to say some words over me!" This was the day. So the funeral was to take place in our church sanctuary, with the interment in a city cemetery some twenty or thirty miles away. The undertakers arrived early that morning with the hearse and a flower van. They had come about twenty miles from a very small-town funeral parlor that for years had occupied an old house on Main Street.

I have noticed that the procedure has been much the same for most funeral directors with whom I have worked: The casket usually stays in place in the coach until all the floral pieces are carried into the church and tastefully arranged. I was standing on the top of the several steps leading up to the front door of the church, which I had been holding open. With all of the flowers delivered and displayed, the owner of the funeral home looked around and counted those of us standing there: "One, two, three, four—I think we can handle it!" All of a sudden, I was included in a group of four temporary pallbearers who were going to attempt to get that casket up the steps and into the building. Having known the deceased, I realized he had been a big, strong man who no doubt stood close to six feet tall. I was also aware that his casket was of solid wood, just as he had requested. Put the two together and you have an extremely heavy combination.

Knowing we needed someone to hold the glass doors open, I ran inside and found my secretary, Michelle. With two of us at the front and two at the back, we pulled the casket out of the hearse and started up the stairs. Was it ever heavy! I hadn't thought about it before we started, but all three of those funeral-home guys were of retirement age! As a matter of fact, the one with me on the rear end stopped abruptly and exclaimed, "My knee's gone out!" He dropped his corner of the coffin, and I did my very best to keep the end off the steps! Each of us holding our part, we had to wait for a moment, while our brother recuperated.

We started again, all of us struggling, the coffin wavering up and down, side to side, until we finally got to the top of the steps. Someone managed to get some wheels underneath, and they wheeled the departed saint into the sanctuary. What a relief! A couple of the guys had to sit for a while. A bit out of breath, I walked over to thank Michelle for holding the doors open. She whispered to me, "I don't know what you're being paid, but it's not enough!"

About that time, the funeral director came quickly into the foyer, asking for, of all things, lighter fluid! He explained that the rough ride up the steps had jostled the body around enough to smear some makeup onto the pale blue lining inside the lid. He said lighter fluid is a "trick of the trade" and will, without a doubt, remove the stain. To honor his request, Michelle looked among the candles and seasonal decorations stored in a closet and came across a small can of lighter fluid. We watched as the master mortician applied the chemical to the casket's lining, and once the spot had dried, sure enough, it was good as new.

As a few members of the family entered the church, the funeral director asked me a serious question: Would I put my car in front of the hearse to escort the procession to the city? Now you have to understand that our church was located out in the country, and we were seldom blessed with police escorts. The longer I thought about it, the more uncomfortable I became about leading this procession. I knew about the dangerous curve on the highway just at the end of our road, and I was also aware of those huge 18-wheelers that so frequently came speeding around that curve every day. I asked my friend if he had a portable flashing red light that he could temporarily put on my car, a practice I had seen before. "No," he replied, "just turn on your headlights!"

Contemplating my dilemma with growing reservation, I walked over to the main glass doors and looked out. To my pleasant surprise, there at the bottom of the steps, parked in front of the hearse was an out-of-town police car. I then remembered that one of the grandsons was a police officer for a nearby town. I quickly found the undertaker and told him of my discovery. We looked into the sanctuary and saw three people paying their respects at the casket, one of them in uniform. I was somewhat relieved when my funeral director friend said, "Let's ask him if he will lead the procession!" We both walked down the church aisle to the front. Apologizing for interrupting their conversation, the funeral director then asked, "Which of you is driving the squad car?" Well, the answer to that question was quite obvious, since two of the men wore suits and the other wore a badge! The policeman in uniform admitted that it was he, and then my friend asked if he would do the honors of leading us to the cemetery. The grandson agreed, adding that he had parked in front of the coach for that very reason. After quite an unforgettable morning, we all arrived at the memorial park that day without incident.

As you can see, sometimes the trip to the cemetery has more winds and bends than there are in the road, but eventually the mourners make it to the final resting place for their beloved. It's the *procession*, that long line of cars, which ensures everyone arrives safely, on time, and together.

10
UNDER THE TENT

"Then his disciples came and took away the body and
buried it, and went and told Jesus" (Matt. 14:12, NKJV).

If I remember correctly, the first funeral I ever officiated was in
third grade. One of the goldfish had been found belly-up in the
class fishbowl, and Mrs. Rowell assigned Jimmy Pefinis and me
to the burial detail. We jumped at the chance, mainly because it
got us out of class for fifteen or twenty minutes. Carrying the life-
less little fish in a wet paper towel, Jimmy and I went outside and
buried it under some tall Georgia pines next to the back fence on
the playground of Gartha B. Peterson Elementary School. But for
some reason, I was not content with just that. I don't think either
of us uttered a word, but I remember looking around in the dirt
until I spotted a green rubber band. Snapping a couple of twigs
off of a small branch that was lying in the leaves, I used the rubber
band to fasten them together until they formed a cross. My friend
snickered as we planted the symbol at the head of the grave, which
would most likely go forever unnoticed, especially since by the next
day it would be trampled away by children at play. During recess
a couple of hours later, Jimmy and I took our teacher to our little
finned-friend's grave. I suppose she was impressed, for the next

time some critter died in class, we were the ones who were again given the honors.

Perhaps we should be reminded that this book is about burying family and friends, not fish. We are not discussing saying good-bye to a pet that might last only a few days. We are instead talking about human beings who make a dent in this world and a difference in our lives. Many times death is an unexpected thing, and we don't have the chance to help a loved one face the dreaded enemy. Then again, there are times when we do have that chance, an opportunity to help a friend or loved one come to terms with his or her own demise. But what about those who are left to mourn? We get off work, we dress in black, we don dark glasses, we have plenty of tissues folded up in our pockets or purses, we lock arms with our family, and we pay our respects.

Jesus of Nazareth was invited to the home of one of the rulers of the synagogue. The official's name was Jairus (Mark 5:22), and his heart had been broken, for his little girl had died. Upon His arrival, Jesus was greeted by all the usual musicians and professional mourners, a common sight at the time of death. Our Lord found it all to be rather disgusting (Matt. 9:23-24). He had other plans for the young lady anyway, plans that included raising her from the dead and restoring life. When someone passes away in our time, the grievers and mourners still gather in. They come to the home, and they are there at the memorial, but the big difference between the two groups separated by time is that the grievers of today are for real. No one is being paid a dime to weep at her mother's funeral. No one is compensated for having a broken heart at the death of his child. Mourners of today have been deeply stabbed with a pain from which they will never recover.

So we attend a viewing and go to a funeral, but what's next? Some people honestly don't know because not everyone joins the procession to the grave site. As a matter of fact, I am always meeting grown adults who tell me they have never been to a funeral. I was surprised at the number of hands raised in a recent seminary class by ministerial students who were admitting they never attended such a service. Just how do we properly dispose of the remains of Uncle Albert, and what is the role of the clergy?

To understand the protocol, let's go back to the procession. Driving our cars in a long line of vehicles, we slowly and reverently approach the cemetery. If there has been a police escort, the officer will speed ahead, stopping in the middle of the street by the entrance of the memorial gardens. He or she will get out of his or her cruiser or dismount the motorcycle and stand at attention as the procession turns through the gate. Usually, a representative of the cemetery is waiting in a car and replaces the police officer as the new leader. The hearse and other vehicles follow the car around the sometimes winding road until they come to the end of the journey. It may be only a few paces away, or it may be several yards away, but nearby there is typically a tent that has been erected over a section of artificial turf, some folding chairs, and the open grave. The trail of flower petals on the ground indicates how swiftly the floral arrangements had been moved from the place of the funeral to the place of the grave while everyone was en route. The fake sod usually hides the fresh dirt and the existence underneath all the mechanical apparatus of a deep hole in the earth that will become a new bed for the remains of someone who was dearly loved.

In the funeral business every attempt is made to cover up the reality of death. I'm not criticizing this attempt. I think it's part of ministering to the bereaved. Fresh flowers fill a state room at the mortuary to bring as much life into the place as possible. (I've never been sure if a funeral home smells like a flower shop or if a flower shop smells like a funeral home!) Makeup, often heavily applied, is a hopeful attempt to make a corpse appear natural and lifelike. Next, placing the remains of a loved one under colored lights, blues and pinks, helps achieve the look that is desired. Later, everything is done to hide the fact that the graveyard is a graveyard. Even the gravediggers and their tractors and trucks are waiting at the other side of the cemetery, sometimes behind a hedge, as if incognito.

Immediately upon the procession's arrival, people begin to exit their cars and the pallbearers all line up just behind the funeral coach. The minister stands close by. The undertaker will give some words of instruction, open the rear door of the hearse (or the side door, if that be the case), and pull out the casket, carefully passing it to the six pairs of hands that will carry the departed to the final resting place. I heard the other day that an elderly lady who never married has requested that her pallbearers be six women. Her reasoning: "When I was alive, the men never took me out, so they're not going to take me out when I'm dead!"

The pastor, walking slowly and often glancing slightly over his or her shoulder to avoid getting too far ahead, leads the coffin carriers around tombstones and between old and new graves toward the waiting tent. A small crowd of mourners follows. Almost without fail, a friendly gravedigger in his work clothes will be standing by the open grave to help position the casket. He's the one I usually approach with my all-important question, "Where's the head?"

A pastor friend of mine told me about the first funeral he officiated as a young minister. This was all so new to him. He approached the grave as the people all moved in. The gravedigger whispered to him words that he thought he heard, "Ed's at the other end." My friend stood there pondering those words, "Ed's at the other end." He told me that he wondered, *Who is Ed, and why do I care where he is?* Then it finally dawned on him that the man had said, "Head's at the other end!"

The gravedigger will tell you the location of the head when you ask, and many times he or she will volunteer this information before you even have a chance to ask. Incidentally, most cemeteries are laid out so that if the deceased were able to sit up, he or she would face the east. This is in anticipation of that great resurrection day when King Jesus will appear in the eastern sky to rapture His Church (Matt. 24:27). Identifying the head of the casket is vital for the minister because that is the end from which he or she will briefly speak.

The Committal Service

Now that everyone and everything is in place, a couple of different kinds of services can take place under the canvas. One is the *committal service,* which is an extension of a funeral service that has already taken place elsewhere. Perhaps the procession just came from the church across town where the funeral was held, or maybe the procession came from the funeral home that had just received the body from a neighboring state where the funeral was held on a previous day.

Once I was sitting in the window seat of a jet, watching the workers just outside. I remember thinking, *No wonder my suitcase is torn up!* as I watched them toss luggage onto the conveyor belt that took the bags up into the belly of the plane. As I continued to watch, I saw them struggle with a long box that they clumsily loaded onto the belt. As the container slowly passed under my window, I could make out some hand-printed letters, the name and address of a funeral home somewhere across the country. I realized the body of someone's loved one was being shipped back home for some kind of disposal, addressed like a parcel to be delivered to a mailbox. My heart went out to a family that would forever remain anonymous. I said a prayer.

Earlier I mentioned that the minister will speak *briefly* at the committal because the sermon has already been delivered. Dr. Armstrong again explains that this cemetery experience should contain

a few words of scripture, the words of committal, a closing prayer, and the benediction, lasting all together about three or four minutes. . . . Say the words with feeling, and directly to the people attending, in the hope that they will actually hear the words of scripture and take to heart your prayer. After the benediction, I usually speak to the family once more and then take my leave. It is best they do not linger too long, for invariably, . . . nearby are the gravediggers, waiting to get to work.[1]

Ministers may purchase books of wedding and funeral rituals at a Christian bookstore, or they may have a denominational manual that gives appropriate words for the occasion. On the shelf of my library is James L. Christenson's *Difficult Funeral Services*.[2] It covers every situation imaginable, from a service for an unidentified decomposed body to that of a naturally aborted baby. Every once in a while, I'll check some of these resources, but in the last few years I've pretty much reverted to speaking from my heart. By the way, much of what takes place at an open grave under a canvas would also transpire inside a mausoleum chapel.

Faith, Hope, and Love

There's a committal ritual I sometimes use, if and when it is fitting. For this to work there must be "a threesome" among the immediate family: A widow and two daughters or three children or a widow and two sisters, and so on. This would not work with a widow and *three* daughters. I arrive under the tent mere moments ahead of everyone else, and I immediately begin searching for flowers. As people are filing in and finding their places, totally unaware of my actions, I pull out three attractive flowers from some of the arrangements that are on display. I don't take them all from the same arrangement because that particular one might be taken home by someone, and I would not want it to be slighted by more than one flower.

When the last few stragglers have made it from their cars and the funeral director nods for me to begin, I start talking about the first flower, one that represents *faith*, faith that someday we'll all be with our loved one again. I then publicly present that flower to one of the threesome. The next flower represents *hope,* and I speak very briefly about the hope of an eternal home, giving the second flower to another of the three. Finally, I spend a moment elaborating on *love,* the love the departed had for the family and vice versa. It is then that I give away the last flower to represent that love. I don't do this often, but every time I have used it, it has been a very meaningful committal for everyone in attendance.

If it is not conducive to do the flower ceremony, I usually begin my remarks by explaining how that beautiful pine box does not hold the real Fred, but only his remains, for Fred left us and went to be with Jesus last Friday afternoon. I tell them how we believe that one day there will be a resurrection of a glorified body that will be reunited with the spirit that had gone on before. Almost always, I read from 1 Cor. 15:

> Behold, I tell you a mystery: We shall not all sleep, but we shall all be changed—in a moment, in the twinkling of an eye, at the last trumpet. For the trumpet will sound, and the dead will be raised incorruptible, and we shall be changed. For this corruptible must put on incorruption, and this mortal must put on immortality. So when this corruptible has put on incorruption, and this mortal has put on immortality, then shall be brought to pass the saying that is written: *"Death is swallowed up in victory." "O Death, where is your sting? O Hades, where is your victory?"* The sting of death is sin, and the strength of sin is the law. But thanks be to God, who gives us the victory through our Lord Jesus Christ *(vv. 51-57).*

At that point I stress to them that the only way we can ever be together again is if we live the life God has intended for us, and I read the next verse of that same passage: "Therefore, my beloved brethren, be steadfast, immovable, always abounding in the work of the Lord, knowing that your labor is not in vain in the Lord"

(v. 58). Those people gathered together are suffering tremendous grief as they mourn the loss of someone who was so dear to them. However, this is not a time to quit. It is not the end of the road. Life goes on, and we will learn to live with the death that has so rattled us. Much is expected of us from God himself, so we must remain immovable, firmly planted in Him.

Asking those attendees to bow their heads, I pray an extemporaneous prayer, including words such as, "And now we tenderly commit the remains of our [brother or sister] to the Lord, knowing [he or she] is already in Your presence. Now in the days ahead, help us to live our lives as ordered by You, so that one day we will be with You for eternity, as well."

What If Deceased Is a Nonbeliever?

If the deceased was not a spiritual person and the whereabouts of that soul is questionable, I will publicly and intentionally commit the remains to the Righteous Judge, leaving him or her in the hands of the One who is merciful. We must keep in mind that we do not have the privilege to judge a person. Although a person may seem to have lived a godless life, it is not up to us to decide his or her fate.

After my final amen, I will step aside so that any military or other rites can be carried out. Once rifles have been fired, taps has been played, and flags have been presented, I will walk to the end of the first row of grievers and, going down the line one by one, I will shake each hand and offer a "God bless you" or "I'll be praying for you." Once I come to the end of that short row, I stand to the side and nod to the funeral director, who makes a statement to conclude the services.

The Graveside Service

A *graveside service* is very similar to a committal service except for a few differences. First of all, a graveside service is usually the only service. A funeral may have taken place somewhere across the miles and now the body is home. Without having another funeral, a graveside service is held for local friends and family who could not attend the other event.

Another possibility is that a graveside service was all that the deceased or the immediate family wanted. Regardless of the reason, the procession to a graveside service may include only a couple of family cars. The funeral coach is there long before anyone arrives, and the casket has already been placed on the lowering device awaiting the mourners. Since there was no funeral (at least in this town), there will most likely be a guestbook on a stand for attendees to sign, acknowledging their presence. The service starts in much the same way as a committal service, but it usually is longer, a mini funeral, as a fitting tribute is made to the departed. There could be a special song. I once saw live doves released from a cage at the end of one such service. At the end of the graveside service, the committal is performed, committing the body into the hands of his or her Creator.

Whether a graveside service or a committal, just as in a hospital setting after a death, and if the weather is decent, no one is going to hurry you along at the cemetery. The casket will stay on the lowering device, and the burial will remain incomplete as long as the mourners linger. It is interesting to me that this "lowering device," as the industry calls it, is usually clutched with a cork braking system so that no matter what caskets weigh by themselves, they all lower into the ground at the same rate.[3]

Clearly, no one desires to see workers burying the remains of their mom or dad or child, and so it is out of respect for both the dead and the living that the officials refrain from their work until the time is appropriate. Once the cars begin to drive away, however, the gravediggers' trucks will quickly converge on a grave site. It is usually the job of the funeral director to remain on the site until he or she sees the grave closed.

When Do You Shorten the Service?

Occasionally, there may be reasons to shorten a committal or graveside service, such as inclement weather or even unnerving circumstances. In chapter 1 I very briefly mentioned a man I buried who had died from an extremely rare malady, at least in our country, eastern equine encephalitis. Hospitalized only a matter of days, his health had declined rapidly, leaving the doctors in a quandary. In his final hours, the uncommon diagnosis was made, but unfortunately, there was no cure. Doctors told us there had been only a few cases of this atypical illness reported in the United States. Evidently, a horse had been suffering with this brain-swelling disease and was bitten by a mosquito, which carried the germ and consequently bit a human being, the man from my church. He suddenly became deathly ill and soon passed away.

It was a hot, sticky summer day when we made the trip to the Outer Banks on the coast of North Carolina. I remember standing under the tent in a cemetery located near some marshland. Awaiting the military salute to be finished, we were all slapping mosquitoes on the backs of our necks, a grim reminder as to why we were there. I think more than a few mourners were ready for the committal to be over so they could get back to their air-conditioned cars.

There have been other times when the weather was such a detriment that we purposely sped things along. A funeral home had asked me to officiate at a graveside service just a few days after Christmas for a stillborn infant. It was bitter cold that morning in El Reno, Oklahoma, and most of the people sat in their cars until it was time to begin. The tent that had been erected in the cemetery was flapping in the wind, which did all but cut a person in two. I could plainly see as the grievers gathered in and huddled together that they were not ready for a lengthy discourse from me. I skipped much of what I had planned to say, prayed, and dismissed the service, all within three or four minutes. Everybody seemed to be satisfied.

Everyone finally leaves the grave site and usually returns to the church for a dinner or perhaps to the home of the immediate family. Many families will return to the closed grave later that day or early evening. Some will come back the next day or within a week or two. Some never return at all. Though I'm only the minister, I have found myself returning to many of these graves a few days or even weeks later. My heart just so goes out to the ones who had suffered the loss. I sometimes go to a cemetery and find all the markers of the graves where I had officiated the services, as best I can remember, and I say a prayer for the families of the deceased.

The Pastor's Work Is Finally Complete . . . or Is It?

Those three to five grueling days between a death and interment are stressful, emotional, and exhausting for everyone involved. After the committal is history, all the people, including the ministers, return to their homes for rest. It's now a chance to relax. No doubt, people will gather in, and for some time that evening there will be laughs and maybe even an opportunity to catch up on the past with those who have been apart. Not too much time should lapse, however, before the preacher visits. A general superintendent in the Church of the Nazarene, the late G. B. Williamson, wrote: "A pastor ought to call in the home of the bereaved at a very early time. In some instances he may go in the evening of the same day the funeral has been held. At other times the next day is better. But promptness in this respect is invariably appreciated."[4] Although Dr. Williamson made that statement a long time ago and the church has admittedly gone through some changes since, I believe what he said still holds true. That initial call after the funeral may be short but better than no visit at all.

11
WHEN IT'S OVER,
IT'S NOT OVER!

"Now Martha said to Jesus, 'Lord, if You had been
here, my brother would not have died'" (John 11:21).

Casseroles are brought to your home for three consecutive days
when there's been a death in your family. You're showered with
cards and even a floral arrangement or two are delivered to you
personally, rather than to the funeral home. Friends and loved ones
visit with hugs, kisses, and words of sympathy. Every act of kind-
ness is meaningful. I remember when I first experienced all this
with my mom's passing in 1973. Then she was buried. Period. No
more visits. A few cards trickled in, but no more flowers or plants.
And whenever my dad, brother, sister, or I ran into friends, even at
church, it was so obvious that everyone tiptoed around us. No one
wanted to mention my mom, and yet her memory was so heavily on
our minds each waking hour of every day.

I guess for most people, once the grave is closed, so is the case.
I understand people are busy and life goes on, and I certainly don't
want to be ungrateful, for I appreciated everything everyone did,
but I think the "being there" needs to taper off over time and not

cease so abruptly. When the committal service is over, it's not really over, at least not for the family in mourning. Others forget, for they've moved on down the road, but the individual who has suffered loss is reminded daily, triggered by some of the most insignificant things.

Just the other day I was running some errands and decided to stop by Taco Bueno for a quick lunch. After I entered the restaurant, it hit me: This was the fast-food place my father-in-law and I frequented for lunch. I would stop by the house around noon on some days and he'd greet me, "Ready for a taco?" Most of the time, plans or not, I couldn't say no, so we went to Taco Bueno and the lady behind the counter always knew his order. As a matter of fact, the last time I had been in that place was with Tom ten months earlier. With all this flooding my mind, I approached the counter, and there she was, that same lady. She took my order but failed to recognize me. I probably should have gone by there after his passing to tell her why she had lost such a faithful customer.

Perhaps sociologist, writer, and lecturer Tony Campolo was right when he quoted his pastor, who was speaking to students at a commencement service: "You don't think you're going to die, but you're going to die. They're going to drop you into a hole. They're going to throw dirt in your face. And they're going to go back to the church and eat potato salad!"[1]

And so life goes on. Everyone is back in the swing of things, sometimes as if nothing was different—except for the ones who have that gaping hole in their hearts.

It's probably unreasonable to expect more from strangers or mere acquaintances, but even some of your closest friends seem to be afraid to mention your departed loved one, as if they are going to set you off and you'll be totally out of control. I remember, though, how I wanted someone to bring up my mom. After my dad was gone, I longed for someone to say something about him. I needed to talk about my parents, and still do. I've enjoyed telling Tommy about the grandparents he never met, and I usually end by saying something such as, "They sure would have loved you, and they would have been so proud of you."

Saying the Wrong Things

We may as well be ready. There are well-meaning people who try to console the bereaved by saying all the wrong things. Some of the more common things said are statements such as these:

1. **"Give it time—you'll get over it!"** But I decided a long time ago that I don't want to get over it! I loved my parents so much that I'll never get over losing them. Even today, some thirty years later, whenever something exciting happens in my life, my first instinct is to call my mom and dad and share the good news! I will learn to cope, and I know the pain will eventually get better, but never will I "get over" them.

2. **"You can have other children"** or **"You can get married again!"** But what about *that* child or what about *that* spouse? They were real people who had feelings and a name. Now they're gone forever, and the one left behind experiences that loss every single day. Well-meaning people do not understand how cruel such a statement is.

3. **"God needed an angel in heaven!"** Usually this is said in response to the death of a child, but how theologically incorrect! The Bible never says that we become angels. As a matter of fact, we have a better deal, for we have a song the angels can't sing—the song of salvation. That reminds me of the most hideous floral arrangement I ever saw at a funeral, somewhere in the South, probably back in the eighties. It was a huge, colorful spray with a plastic telephone mounted in the center. The receiver was off the hook and the ribbon banner read, "God called, Bob answered!"

4. **"There's a reason for everything!"** That's right—put the

blame on God! I am convinced that God is not a giant Puppeteer in the sky who pulls all our strings as if we were a bunch of marionettes. I don't believe for a second that everything takes place for a reason and will teach us some great lesson in life. I do believe that God can take the bad and turn it into good, but He doesn't cause everything to happen.

5. "It's been six months—why are you still upset?" Those who make such a declaration have obviously never suffered loss. They have never stared at the empty chair at a table. They have never listened to the sometimes deafening silence when one sits at home alone. They have never done the little things, such as write the tithe check or take out the trash or check the locks on the doors at night, after someone else had done those things for forty years.

6. "Oh, I know how you feel!" In most cases, only God knows how the griever feels. We may *sympathize* with people, which means our hearts go out to them and we feel sorrow for them, but we can never *empathize* with them until we've been in their place. And even then, if we have suffered a loss ourselves, it is still never the same as that of someone else. So we may never be able to fully know how a person feels during his or her time of grief.

Good Grief

We need to realize that grief is not wrong. Dr. Charles A. Corr, a specialist on the subject of death and dying, wrote, "Grief is a normal and healthy response to loss. It would be abnormal and unhealthy not to respond to a significant loss in one's life."[2] We should also be aware that grief includes various stages that people experience. Though not the official stages of grief that psychologists recognize, here are a few random feelings that some mourners go through:

1. **Self-pity.** Some people mope around, feeling so sorry for themselves, that they drive their friends and relatives away. No one

wants to be with them because of their numerous pity parties. They experience what I like to call the Elijah syndrome, where all they want to do is crawl up under a broom tree and die because they feel they've been left all alone! (1 Kings 19:4).

2. **Anger.** One reaction of grievers is anger. "Why did he have to suffer that heart attack and leave me to take care of the kids?" "Why did she have to leave me when everything was so great in our lives?" Anger is especially seen in cases of suicide, usually viewed as a very selfish act.

One lady had lost her husband to brain cancer at the age of thirty-eight. At the encouragement of the hospital staff during her husband's illness, she kept a journal that included both her writings and some drawings. One drawing was an outline of a woman with a huge opened mouth, screaming the words in all caps, "NOOO—I WASN'T READY!" The same words were repeated smaller and smaller and smaller down her body.[3] It was a self-portrait illustrating her pain.

3. **Blame.** Many people tend to blame God for the loss of life, as Martha did Jesus. In her eyes, had Jesus come when they called, her brother would not have been entombed. Believers tend to feel that God is the Creator (and He is) and that He can intervene when He desires (and He does). At the same time, there are occasions when He chooses not to provide the miracle we're after and allows nature to take its course. Thus God gets the blame.

Or perhaps, another person is blamed. The deceased is gone because of the stress he or she was under from his or her spouse. He is gone because of the driver of that other car. She's gone because he failed to call for help in time. On and on go the excuses as hurting people play the blame game.

4. **Guilt.** As a pastor, many times I have seen grown people weep uncontrollably because of what they did or what they didn't do. Maybe they didn't come around often enough. Perhaps they

had a big fight with the deceased the week before the passing. I have seen some who had not spoken in years to the person, and now that he or she is gone, the guilt has set in.

For the Goddard household, 2006 was not the best year. After eleven weeks in the hospital and a few more weeks in a nursing home, we lost my father-in-law on the first of May. Tom Waldrep was a quiet but radiant Christian man who loved Jesus with all his heart. He told me on my ordination day that it was the greatest day of his life. Tom and I had become great friends, and we enjoyed having lunch together and discussing the church. After his wife, Juanita, suffered a fatal heart attack, Tom moved into the parsonage with us in Yukon, Oklahoma. There we had four wonderful years together.

A few months after Tom was gone, we lost our ninety-three-year-old Aunt Gene. Eugenia Stahly was the widow of a retired Nazarene minister, Rev. Elmer Stahly. Aunt Gene never had children of her own, so Sandie became her caretaker. She spent the last months in the same nursing facility as Tom.

In between those two losses, Sandie, Tommy, and I made the difficult decision to put Bingo down. Bingo was our black Lab, the best pup we had ever had. It was in an Indiana preschool that Tommy learned the song "A big black dog sat on a back porch and Bingo was his name-o." So Bingo was the present we gave Tommy for his fifth birthday. We covered a box in gift wrap and put that little black pup inside with a ribbon and tag around his neck that read, "My name is Bingo!" We have a video of Tommy removing the lid and jumping back when that tiny black head popped out.

Sandie and I had lost a previous pet, so I was bound and determined not to become attached to this one. My plan, however, was sabotaged. Once while my family was away and I was home alone, a tornado developed near Muncie, Indiana. Having no basement in the parsonage, our place of escape was the basement of the church's fellowship building just across the parking lot. I put a leash on Bingo that night and dragged that trembling dog down the steps into the basement of that building. As we waited out the storm together, we bonded.

Tommy and Bingo grew up together. The pup got bigger first, many times playfully dragging Tommy across the backyard by the cuff of his jeans. Then Tommy grew taller and older but still made time for his pup. Bingo developed arthritis and the drugs ceased to be effective. We took him to the vet, and the three of us held him, petted him, loved him, and wept over him as his fourteen and a half years came to an end. This was by far the hardest thing I had ever done, and the feelings of my family were mutual. The doctor assured us we were doing the right thing—but we weren't so sure. We grappled with what we had done for the next few days, weeks, and months. We still look back to that summer day and wonder if we had done the right thing. Even though he was unable to walk and move around without help during those last few weeks, we could look into his eyes and see Bingo was still there. I guess we'll always have some remorse.

Jesus was met by a father one day whose son was severely ill with some form of epilepsy. Our Lord assured the man that anything was possible to those who believe, and the man made a startling, yet honest confession: "I do believe, Lord, but way down deep inside is a little bit of doubt—please, help me with that unbelief!" (Mark 9:24, author's paraphrase). It may be that weeks, perhaps months, after losing your loved one, you are still plagued with guilt: "I should have spent more time with her," and so on. Guilt will eat you alive. We must gain control. We must commit it to God. We must allow the Holy Spirit to help us here.

5. **Regrets.** Pretty much hand in hand with guilt is regrets. I suppose I fall into this category. In October 1975 at the coaxing of my pastor, I decided to attend college in Nashville. At the same time, I was feeling a call to preach, something about which I told

no one, except Pastor Dudney. On a Sunday night just after Christmas that same year, my dad suddenly passed away in our home. His funeral was on Wednesday, I packed all day Thursday, and I started classes at Trevecca Nazarene College on Friday. It was in February 1976 that I accepted God's call in a revival Dr. Talmadge Johnson was preaching in Atlanta. I had prayed for six months and had to be sure, but I will always regret never telling my dad that I thought God had chosen me to be a preacher.

6. **Fear.** It can be a scary thing when someone has suddenly been left alone. What will happen to such a person? Who will take care of him or her? Many times a widow has to wonder about such things as mowing the lawn or taking care of the car or reroofing the house.

What Can We Do to Help?

Ministers and caregivers need to realize the agony with which grieving people are struggling. The funeral may be done, but the pastor is not, according to Richard Stoll Armstrong, professor of ministry and evangelism at Princeton:

Your pastoral services to the bereaved family do not end with the funeral. It is important to keep in touch, as the most difficult time for many bereaved persons comes weeks and even months after the death, when the shock has subsided and reality has set in, and when the sharp pain of grief becomes the dull ache of loneliness.[4]

Certainly personal visits, phone calls, and notes or cards are always in order. If you are a pastor or even a good friend, keep close contact with the one who is mourning a loss. One thing I do as a pastor is send letters to immediate family members at different times throughout the grieving process. Here is a sample of a letter that I send out on the first anniversary of a death:

Dear Randy and Robin,

I just wanted you to know that I am very much aware this is

the month you are experiencing the first anniversary of the loss of Robin's sister in Colorado. I know you cherish fond memories of her and will hold her in your hearts forever.

The past twelve months have not been easy for you, I'm sure. No doubt, you have discovered many adjustments along the way, but these are nonetheless difficult days for you and your family. It may be helpful to keep in mind the Words of our Savior, *"Peace I leave with you, My peace I give to you. . . . Let not your heart be troubled, neither let it be afraid"* (*John 14:27*). I trust you can find rest in an assurance that your dear sister is enjoying the presence of Jesus.

I have remembered you in prayer this month. May the Comforter continue to bring comfort to you and yours as you remember days gone by.

For Him,

Danny Goddard

In addition to the first anniversary letter, I have similar letters filed away on the computer for other pertinent times, such as six-month or five-year anniversaries. In order to send these letters, my secretary keeps track of significant deaths in the lives of our people. Then at the end of each month, she leaves in my mailbox a list of people who had experienced a loss during that next month. The letter indicates if the deceased was a parent or child, a brother, sister, an in-law, and so on. The date of death is also included, so I will know whether to send the two-year letter or the five. When I first started doing this, the heading at the top of the list was "Pastor's Death List." Fearing it might fall into the wrong hands, I changed the document's heading to "Pastor's Bereavement List."

His Amazing Sufficient Grace

You and I have heard people say with dread, "I would never be able to make it if I ever lost him or her." We don't even want to go there, for the idea is much too painful. But sometimes that day does come and we do suffer that loss. Over the years, I have stood by and watched how people do what they thought they could never do—they make it through the difficulty of death. How do they do it?

I have always preached about the amazing grace of God. I've preached how God provides for us a saving grace, a sanctifying grace, a sustaining grace, and all of that begins with a prevenient grace. But then I've witnessed *an amazing sufficient grace* that is God provided, but only when needed. It's a grace an individual cannot obtain beforehand. It's only available at the time of loss. When a person dies, the believer who is left behind immediately receives an abundance of this grace that enables him or her to cope with the demands of the hour. What a mighty God we serve!

Dr. James Dobson spent one evening in 1987 with four close friends. The next day their private plane never made it to Dallas. Dr. Dobson was asked to speak at two of the funerals and, in preparation, searched for answers. As they exited the church, they immediately saw a rainbow in the sky. I'll let the doctor unfold the rest:

It was as though the Lord was saying to the grieving wives and children, "Be at peace. Your men are with Me, and all is well. . . .

One of the people standing there had the presence of mind to take a photograph. When it was developed, we saw what no one had recognized at the time. There, cradled near the center of the rainbow, was a small private plane.[5]

God is ever about taking care of His children and even in the midst of such a tragedy, He finds ways to communicate to us that He is providing His amazing sufficient grace.

So when the viewing, the funeral, the procession, and the burial are all history, most people think everything is finished. But for the pastor, the caregiver, the best friend, and the family member, it is only the beginning of helping someone to cope.

Tam Lytle, a children's pastor in Kansas, recently lost Tom, her husband of twenty-one years. Tom had been diagnosed with brain cancer, and although his prognosis included more time, after ten months of treatment, he lost his battle, leaving behind a wife and two sons. Tam is pleased to share the list of thirteen things that are helping her to cope with her loss. I won't elaborate on them, for I think each is self-explanatory.

1. Pray.
2. Read and recall the Bible.
3. Cry.
4. Accept help.
5. Maintain routines.
6. Focus on others.
7. Stay connected.
8. Stay active.
9. Treasure memories.
10. Listen to Christian music.
11. Take a walk or a drive in the car.
12. Remember.
13. Be thankful.[6]

That Cloud of Witnesses

We are all probably familiar with the Bible verse that describes our being surrounded by "so great a cloud of witnesses" (Heb. 12:1). I like *The Living Bible*'s paraphrase: "a huge crowd of men of faith watching us from the grandstands." The idea is that those who have gone on to heaven before us are now encouraging us to live the Christian life, to "run the race," so that we, too, will make it all the way to the finish line, as did they, and thus we can all be together again.

Countless people believe that our departed loved ones are watching over us, seeing all that we do. I'm not sure about a lot of that. I do believe that when Christians die, their spirits go immediately into the presence of Jesus, and I also believe that we will know one another in glory. Paul wrote, "For now we see in a mirror, dimly, but then face to face. Now I know in part, but then I shall know just as I also am known" (1 Cor. 13:12).

It is also my strong opinion that each of us needs to come to some theological conclusion on our own about the afterlife. Pastor David Busic believes doing so will make a difference: "Your belief in the afterlife and your belief in the resurrection will change your life here and now."[7] No matter what we believe personally, our departed loved ones will continue to be real in our thoughts and memories. Just because the grave is closed and the cars are gone does not mean it's all said and done in the hearts, minds, and lives of those left behind.

CONCLUSION
OL' BUDDY BOY

"Then I said, "Here am I! Send me" (Isa. 6:8).

He was a relative of a family in my church, and I called on him a couple of times but didn't really know him. Off and on, he had attended a church of another denomination, and I knew that pastor was calling on him as well. Having lung cancer, our friend was coming to the end of life. It was sometime after midnight when I received "the phone call," and I rushed to the hospital to be with the family from my congregation. Since I had had a small part in their dad's life, they asked me to be one of two pastors officiating at the funeral.

Prayerfully, I found what I believed was God's direction, and I prepared my message. On the eve of the service, a phone call from a daughter brought a special request. It seemed that no one knew her father by his real name. People were even missing the obituary in the newspaper because they did not recognize the name that was listed. So the family asked that every time I refer to their father in my message that I use the nickname with which everyone was so familiar. Of course, the wishes of the family are a minister's command, so I inquired about the nickname. "Ol' Buddy Boy," she replied. Writing this down, I asked, "Old Buddy Boy?" "No," she corrected me, "*Ol'* Buddy Boy."

I guess I felt it just a little peculiar to refer to someone with whom I was barely acquainted by such an endearing pet name.

151

Funeral time came and I remember how the church was packed out that afternoon, no doubt 300 people in attendance. Reverently, I began my remarks, "We are here this afternoon to remember Ol' Buddy Boy!" I did exactly as I was asked, calling this gentleman Ol' Buddy Boy throughout the entire message. Now I'll admit that each time I called him such, I was a little tickled, but I noticed how everyone else was greatly touched.

Later, we were at the cemetery and I had just finished the committal service under the tent. One by one, teary-eyed individuals came to me, voicing their sentiments about the departed. "I've known Ol' Buddy Boy over forty years," one gentleman told me. Another exclaimed, "Ol' Buddy Boy and I go way back!" That's when I realized something for the first time that would help me for the rest of my days: Every person we ministers lay to rest, even those we never had the privilege of knowing, is an "Ol' Buddy Boy" to someone.

So treat them with dignity and respect. Be a friend to the dying and guide them through their final days. Be there for the grievers, letting your words be limited, and walk the lonely path with them. Pull out all the stops and give them the best funeral you possibly can. Make it personal and keep it simple. Allow God's Holy Spirit to use you to touch the life of someone who is hurting. Whether you are a pastor, lay minister, or a good friend, if you will do these things, God will bless you in your ministry to the mourning.

NOTES

Introduction
1. Alden Sproull, "Hospital Ministry with Cancer Victims," *Preacher's Magazine,* March/April/May 1986, 39.

2. Eugene H. Peterson, *Living the Resurrection* (Colorado Springs, Colo.: NavPress, 2006), 89.

Chapter 1
1. Emily Dickinson, The Quote Garden, http://www.quotegarden.com/death.html (accessed November 11, 2008).

2. Robert Alton Harris, The Quote Garden, http://www.quotegarden.com/death.html (accessed November 11, 2008). ·

3. Robert Anderson, *The Effective Pastor* (Chicago: Moody Bible Institute, 1985), 255.

4. Harold Ivan Smith, *When Your People Are Grieving* (Kansas City: Beacon Hill Press of Kansas City, 2001), 9.

5. Mark Twain, The Quote Garden, http://www.quotegarden.com/death.html (accessed November 11, 2008).

Chapter 2
1. Anderson, *Effective Pastor,* 254.

2. Eugene L. Stowe, *The Ministry of Shepherding* (Kansas City: Beacon Hill Press of Kansas City, 1976), 96.

3. Smith, *When Your People Are Grieving,* 21.

4. Jeren Rowell, *What's a Pastor to Do?* (Kansas City: Beacon Hill Press of Kansas City, 2004), 88.

5. Referenced in Charlotte Lankard, "Remembering Child Key to Dealing with Loss," *Daily Oklahoman,* May 29, 2006, 1B.

6. Jan Johnson, "Weeping with God," *Pray! Magazine,* May/June 2006, 12.

7. Smith, *When Your People Are Grieving,* 97.

Chapter 3
1. Jim Diehl, "A Day in the Life of a General Superintendent: Never the Same Day Twice," *Holiness Today,* August 2003, 15.

2. Stan Toler, *The People Principle* (Kansas City: Beacon Hill Press of Kansas City, 2003), 121.

3. Smith, *When Your People Are Grieving,* 32.

4. Bill M. Sullivan, *New Perspectives on Breaking the 200 Barrier* (Kansas City: Beacon Hill Press of Kansas City, 2005), 16.

Chapter 4

1. Tim Adams (Mercer-Adams Funeral Service, Bethany, Oklahoma), in telephone conversation with the author, May 15, 2006.

2. Andrew W. Blackwood, *The Funeral* (Grand Rapids: Baker Book House, 1942), 157.

Chapter 5

1. Alan Wolfelt, *Creating Meaningful Funeral Ceremonies: A Guide for Caregivers* (Fort Collins, Colo.: Companion Press, 1994), 7.

2. O. Duane Weeks, "Using Funeral Rituals to Help Survivors," in *Living with Grief After Sudden Loss*, ed. Kenneth J. Doka (Bristol, Pa.: Taylor and Francis, 1996), 132.

3. Smith, *When Your People Are Grieving*, 97.

4. Dr. Les Parrott III, "Laugh It Up!" *Holiness Today*, July/August 2005, 10.

5. Ibid.

6. Anderson, *Effective Pastor*, 258-59.

7. Stowe, *Ministry of Shepherding*, 97.

8. Anderson, *Effective Pastor*, 260-61.

9. Weeks, "Using Funeral Rituals to Help Survivors," 133.

Chapter 6

1. *Webster's Online Dictionary*, s.v. "Funeral," http://www.websters-online-dictionary.org/definition/funeral (accessed November 12, 2008).

2. Thomas C. Oden, *Pastoral Theology* (San Francisco: HarperCollins, 1983), 309.

3. Dan Boone, *Answers for Chicken Little* (Kansas City: Beacon Hill Press of Kansas City, 2005), 59.

Chapter 7

1. Anderson, *Effective Pastor*, 261.

2. Marva Dawn and Eugene Peterson, *The Unnecessary Pastor* (Grand Rapids: William B. Eerdsman Publishing Co., 2000), 219.

3. Stan Toler, *Stan Toler's Practical Guide for Pastoral Ministry* (Indianapolis: Wesleyan Publishing House, 2007), 113.

Chapter 8

1. Richard Stoll Armstrong, *The Pastor-Evangelist in Worship* (Philadelphia: Westminster Press, 1986), 61.

2. Dr. Millard Reed, sermon at First Church of the Nazarene, Nashville, 1977.

Chapter 9

1. Grant McKenzie, "How Safe Are Funeral Processions?" www.TheFuneral Directory.com, http://www.thefuneraldirectory.com/procession.html (accessed January 8, 2009).

2. David Busic, "What Christians Believe About What Happens When We Die," Part 2 (sermon, Bethany First Church of the Nazarene, Bethany, Oklahoma, Sunday night, November 29, 2006).

Chapter 10
1. Armstrong, *Pastor-Evangelist in Worship*, 71.
2. James L. Christenson, *Difficult Funeral Services* (Old Tappan, N.J.: Fleming H. Revell Co., 1985).
3. Tim Adams (Mercer-Adams Funeral Service, Bethany, Oklahoma), in telephone conversation with the author, December 11, 2006.
4. G. B. Williamson, *Overseers of the Flock* (Kansas City: Beacon Hill Press, 1952), 136.

Chapter 11
1. Dr. Tony Campolo, "Glancing Backward, Looking Forward: The Intersection of Culture and Religion" (lecture, Wake Forest University, Winston Salem, N.C., January 22, 1998).
2. Dr. Charles A. Corr, "Someone You Love Is Dying. How Do You Cope?" in *Picking Up the Pieces* (Service Corporation International, 1992), 22.
3. Ibid., 5.
4. Armstrong, *Pastor-Evangelist in Worship*, 72.
5. James Dobson, "Solid Answers," *Focus on the Family* magazine, September 2002, 5.
6. Tam Lytle, "Facing Loss," *Holiness Today*, March/April 2005, 34.
7. Busic, "What Christians Believe About What Happens When We Die" (November 29, 2006).

ABOUT THE AUTHOR

Danny Goddard is a graduate of Trevecca Nazarene University in Nashville. He has a master's degree in church management from Olivet Nazarene University and a master of divinity degree from Nazarene Theological Seminary in Kansas City. He has pastored Churches of the Nazarene in Indiana, Nebraska, North Carolina, and Oklahoma. Danny and Sandie have one son, Tommy.

Danny Goddard officiating a grave site service
in a national cemetery in Pineville, Louisiana.